THE CHOREOGRAPHER:
COURT OF RECORD

KWAYANI ROSEUS

authorHOUSE®

AuthorHouse™
1663 Liberty Drive
Bloomington, IN 47403
www.authorhouse.com
Phone: 1 (800) 839-8640

Published by AuthorHouse 09/12/2019

ISBN: 978-1-7283-2676-4 (sc)
ISBN: 978-1-7283-2675-7 (e)

SHADOWS IN HISTORY

Femininity is like a voided space.
Shadows are its single blessing.
Experienced space here is a miniature
Image of our memory;
Corners between two walls
where wood meets wood.
Images of a secret stronger than sound
And lighter than death

Kimberly A. Barker CD

CONTENTS

NOTES TO WRITINGS

I wrote these poems after researching the approach of one residential property to that of another through a contractor in Prince Edward Island. I also live in a city which is home to the Communications and Electronics Branch of the Canadian Armed Forces at CFB Kingston collectively called Poets trades whose acquaintance recalls some very vulgar NICS toward our personally gifted presence especially to the art and architecture of the home as opposed to the seat of parliament.

In Muslim tradition, mythologies of Middle East cultures are used to gain power within religious constituents, such as the one Muslim student with an aura of O'Sama Bin Ladin found at a checkout in a downtown Shoppers Drug Mart. Religious extremists who are martyrs for Islam will assume these hatreds against all Canadian descendants using the social insurance number system against their parents here in Ontario. She may not have even realized the danger about his presence at the time the threat was made. However, since I've had some insight into these writings, the protection for her is almost always as short lived as was the danger to expose her dictatorial option. The message signified then and there was to firmly state that Canada, where we all pay our taxes, is that Christianity will take precedence in the Courts over Islam or Judaism. Besides knowing this, the greatest danger to all living organisms belong to the safety of our natural resources; not the global infrastructure of her faith per se.

The preoccupations for me now with these mythologies that are uniquely connected to the seclusion of my own father upon himself as a memory to the Royal Newfoundland Regiment of WWI, where it is written in legal seal to the constitution of Canada, that the past aversion of this City proves no concealment to a vehement hatred toward me with details of more powerful dangers awaiting us under the threat of war in the future of Canada. Notwithstanding an in-depth analysis was required to support that theory. Thus, poetry had to be the formal research required to tap into an objective authority.

Jinni or genie literally mean anything that has the connotation of concealment, invisibility, seclusion or remote foreignness. They are supernatural creatures that are ranked below the level of God and Angels. Furthermore, as a point to offer myself in this report, is the titled symbol "Abegweit Flight Path" that shows the destruction of an whole history to the name of Princess of Snowdon through the Dead Poet's Society.

Since these jinn too are mythological subjects and can take on the form of animals as well as humans, they are most often used in exchange for money by occultists for whom they may be summoned to influence by divorce, bad luck, ill health or other unplanned disasters. They are believed to have been made by God from what is called a smokeless fire such as fog or dew, in contrast for instance to Adam and Eve who were made from the clay of the earth. They can settle anywhere from tiny holes to huge vast expanses and even sometimes, accidentally or deliberately, come into view or contact with humans.

Pluralistically, they are called Djinn from which there are four classifications: Ghouls are treacherous spirits, night shades that can change shape, yet are relatively harmless. Next are the Si'la which cannot change shape yet are nonetheless very treacherous in a supernatural kind of way. Then there are the I'frit which are decidedly diabolical spirits in an evil way such as how the Moslem portrayed herself to me. Lastly, there are the Marid forms which are the strongest of the Jinni. These are the ones that have me worried most about the male lineages to the Newfoundland Regiment in my own father's testament.

Another source associates the Djinn with open waters of the seas and oceans where it finds sanctuary. They also can grant wishes to mortals in which the other classes of jinni do not. However, like the Monkey's Paw story, they are normally forced to do battle with the Djinn. While others describe the Marid's power as leaving a trail like sludge, my real grandmother in the biological sense of lineages to the Princess of Snowdon, is proof that death is an unforgivable truth to the living.

Since these mythologies have been sourced in this area, I have a bias of never trusting the riding of the Islands ever again. Economically speaking, it is just too H.G. Wells for this artist living in the local vicinity of magnolias prescriptions. The good news is that my only son is alive.

CHAPTER ONE

STYLE HOME DESIGN

As for the donations given in death, remember that no matter how much you give or take, it will not be enough for the wager of law.

Ab sit omen was the last thing she entered on the minutes of the meeting on behalf of the Command. If there is no Canadian content she figured, then there can be no protection by the law. Furthermore, she didn't have an advertisement in any city to compare sandstorms against snowstorms and the absolutism was above board with their American counterparts. The only thing left to relate to now when the monetary system engaged the obituary, was the Aurora Borealis feature within the northern landscapes. Its theory however was still trying to establish itself within the scientific community. She also knew it was far-fetched when it came to moral obligations or institutional associations. A5 was as close as she could get to a call sign. Yet it seemed lame next to the longest standing dossier established to her knowledge as "Tawnge."

The deprivation of talents was within the ecumenical governance of this person to the family of names to the Princess of Snowdon. Her father relied on the discipline in training centers across Canada to gain access to public archives of personnel. She, his file sharing dictate, was without proof to the scandalous administrations offered by the regime of jealously to a pay scale. In the marriage contract, it was Liberalism without passion. He knew they placed the title unemployed in the documentation on behalf of the Royal visits to Canada in the four eyes of contracts to the business of government dictations. Now the extreme fourth dimensional approach was the military campaign to assert on behalf of the people, specifically to the cultural participant. The mole was maintaining his presence with a capitalistic budget of taxation to the people of Quebec using telephone numbers to criminalize family members of their vehicular accidents over a period of time.

Since she memorized everyone's personal attaché of residential account, it was easy to agitate the system of administration to the police account. It just didn't have to be the residue of training women specifically to an assault charge just because the army has its training manuals assigned to men at the artillery gate of the forming of our country. With the art of fictive spaces, she could easily engage trading partners. It also was the truth. She remembered she had to get permission from the author's publishers in order to correct the mistake that had been made. It was just an interpretation and even though there was no harm in the correctness per se, it was as venomous as a plumber's crack to see how many people would try to break into his room. Personally, as well, she had never felt it was necessary to challenge anything that wasn't already in print. The jinn, in the attempt to claim her writing as the poet reminded her of the legacy where she knew of a fraudster in a plagiarized literary work from the United States. These circumstances belonged to such Special Markets Departments of Publishers in the city of New York in the state of New York where there are a great many broken-hearted proletarians. Considering that fact alone, made the presentation vulnerable to accelerated canons.

She then changed the focus that pondered the idea that Anna Lane was somehow associated with Anabaptism and the canoness. This notion was a Bel for the marker. Parades come in many forms for which the ball would be used to misplay the score for more than one soldier on campus. The number seventy-five had to be diffused. The unknown soldier would not suffer the ecumenical debate. The A5 call sign was obscure enough to be considered a fact to weigh in as her registration. Satisfied that the conventions of any city supporting the bill, it became the gift worth repeating on the coin. It was also completely within her public domain as the author and not the fraud of the same publication of poets' names. How could anyone despise her for all that? There is nothing abnormal in the use of an abscissa to make the obelisk invisible and therefore AWOL.

They had no other choice but to pay her. It was not a consignment either that they were talking about. Supplier labels read as symbols as well as workplace labels. It also had nothing to do with construction notes and she knew very well that labels were the first part of the delivery system. For example, supplier labels are placed on containers while the employers are responsible for workplace labels such as signs on doors and mail delivery services to those contracts for government use. For her to make her workplace known was to devise a label that would conform to the specifications of a manufacturing design if a supplier went missing or was illegible. It made sense of every abstract she encountered on economic theory to the Julien calendar of military soldiers.

What was even more delightful was realizing that the recognition of just one single letter could be presented in both English and French without any distinctive border. The CGEP program had to realize the use of colour coded tags suitable to let workers know what materials were contained in their pipes of distribution for military aircraft as opposed to Air Canada employees. Now that the transportation of dangerous goods legislation allowed for the transport of goods by air, water, road or rail in Canada and by employing the Transportation of Dangerous Goods Act, one system could provide where another system did not seem needed to exist. Again, the word ab sit omen appears to protect the innocent.

Video based, self-study programs went together with the NATO number C-54-818-000/MS-0E0 where there is created an employment title. However, the sponsors of the training program did not give the participants any value for their safety concerns. The advancement of personnel was dictated by the language experts of both official languages and the corruption of advancement went to the male lineages first from the MAMS or traffic airfield-based pilots. The point of allowing mentally challenged persons a civilian position and seniority status also contributed to the demise of the organization. To her it was one thing to know the risks of the dangerous goods act, yet it is quite another thing to have to secure your person against dangerous men who would not know the difference of whether or not they were cognitive of their motor skills and were physically capable of killing someone. The result of this experience was a written report to her section supervisor stating that he had pushed her from behind as she was looking over the balcony waiting to receive the stores for the company's pantry.

Just as there are groupings of categories of occupancy, there are classes of people for the workplace which in her opinion, should not be there due to their hazardous nature of behaviors. While there are classes of symbols for hazardous materials, there are also classes of fire extinguishers and building code occupancies. While class A refers to compressed gas and group A refers to assembly occupancy such as rooms, studios and theatres and Class C symbols refer to things like hydrogen peroxide which when combined with flammable materials may cause skin and eye burns. First aid volunteers are not trained to figure out the response to an hostile business takeover from the Group C category of residential occupancy with an atelier that may or may not be associated with oxidizing materials. If the administration of the detail design proved to be colour based on real light emissions, she would refer to ancient light for the room's design from the general contractor as opposed to the cell of the architectural detail of the local police holding cells.

As much as there is an understanding to both systems, the fact remains that the divisions are still categorized from one postal code system to another. Furthermore, they are not uniquely written in either English or French as a distinctive symbol. Hitherto, music has always been written from a recognized array of languages that read from left to right wherein moments of wonder, ecstasy, pain and yes even solitary contempt, enlighten a sited individual. As agents to market, she would be the first to capitalize on such an unique distinctive symbol for this type of workplace protection plan for her only son. My office is a group C and D parcel. The C which accompanies the marketing of talent includes absolutely the quality of status to accompany individuals as they move about the country.

A major occupancy is the Division Design Officer. It is a veto over the gender analysis of the cast of actors to a copyrighted play. As workers, rights and responsibilities include the right to refuse unsafe work and to consult with professionals on the hazards they may be exposed to as employed by any omitted label identifiers. Since there are no protections for volunteers, a policy may be in violation of a named safety representative for the workplace. However, with the use of a sign on the premises, the designation of a safety officer is always in order.

The account was selected to reflect this premise. Those benefits, in return, belong to everyone working with implementation of an appropriate emergency procedure. At this fact of understanding life, Mormonism is inappropriate to the Canadian Constitution and our law to behavioral sciences on a personal level. Therefore, it is not a condition of Canadian workplace specific education for residential occupancies especially if they have been deemed unqualified to read in either English or French.

As part of an elected group of members to the Board of Trustees in a regional riding, it was my privilege to weigh in on some of the folklore, legends and romances of our military elite. The Captain here was a Middle East character in the promotion of Palestinian women and I was stuck divided in the political history of the Trudeau brand. Pierre

Laporte Middle School was already programmed in these arrangements of solicitation of our children and it followed into our land ownerships of those educational ministries of charitable organizations. The fact that the Reverend conducted his certification of baptisms unscrupulously was my truth to first names verses sir names.

Elaine is part of a select list of names. She has something in common with Sheri, Greg, Donna, Erwin, and Moshen. It is from old English. It may not be as far back as the legend of Beowulf but far enough back to feel the romance of Sir Lancelot and her death as she pines away for a lover who would never have children. She was the first of signatories to the family bible. This is a classic ballad as rich as any opera and still today I have been interested in every version that has ever been produced for public debate. My adjustment to the Tess of Thomas Hardy is similar.

The Reverend's name was Thomas. Thomas the Rhymer was a Scottish magician, prophet and poet. He was sometimes referenced by his contemporary William, as the Merlin of Scotland. Avalon is linked to this man's myth in Canada through the classic tale written by Lucy Maud Montgomery. There is a world of difference between these literary works with those of H.G. Wells. Green Gables of Avalon being the Elysium for the forests of Arthurian legend that growled in Celtic honour. K stands for kindness in the encouragement of free thinking among the currency of nations.

In another world of legends and romance, there exists a Kriemhild, or sister to a King. In legendary terms, her vengeance is unforgiveable even today for the loss of her husband. Today, we are offered the budget of a midwife for the clinical psychology for this type of obsolete debate as though the situation existed for all tenured officers. Graham Greene wrote many stories that were as equally treacherous to the constitutions of women and death. My first analysis of writing in public for this experience in English was with the MacJanet word processing application as opposed to the database management of military personnel for a Professor Gregory. She was far from being a Goddess of the university library whose fates determined the birth, life and death of man. As for her first name, it didn't matter so much as the fact that her last name was the first of many men of the Papacy. This brought me into the Roman interpretation of the rise and fall of empires from my scholarship Athena, goddess of wisdom, to do battle with the equated Minerva of Roman literature.

I was very much aroused to delve into these minds of authors at the time of my research since the Aurora was an aircraft of the Atlantic services for the unit of my posting. As it was read, the representation of two children from old testament, who lived on the street were also in the category of one male and one female. They had always been seeking refuge, as children, in the homes of the well to do and educated classes of the urban setting. Not much wonder why we were challenged by the career managers of the Ottawa administrations. Living on the streets meant that the old worlds and new worlds could potentially rise and fall again without warning. Yet, I wondered why they would act on an impulse to her performance records of being a professional logistics deed of the Federal capacity for hire?

As for the meeting with the Cotton sir name, here is a little gossip to internationalize the sacrilegious Hodges from European exchange programs for children finishing high school and not elementary school. In certain training exercises, administrations were computerized to introduce sexual denotations to children prior to reaching their goals of ownership to land titles. My recollection of Lady Diana Spencer to the Prince Charles of the next in line to the throne took place after both my children were born and their certificates to have been obtained by me from the Department of Vital Statistics to the Province of Nova Scotia. Thus, in the lettering of oaths to the people of Canada, why is it that the mother, me, to my children being systematically demoted to street imps when the land is registered to her motto "Veritas Vincit" and to the educated classes of founding provinces within Canadian Law and Business within Confederation and not of history. Equally irregular to mathematical disclosure was the journalism of my CV to the lineage of Prince William to a baptism appearing on the records of Church authority to a falsified document by the Reverend Thomas with children Josh and Sarah.

Now the Atlantic Ocean was my ownership aura and glory for my children as well. I loved the sea with its many colours and the myth of my personal favorite legends of Atlantis. I wanted both my children very much to grasp some of its essence which began my journey into the oils of ancient light so that they too could cultivate some of the natural beauty of our east coast landscapes. Atlantis, as differentiated from the "Island of Dr. Moreau" and the Moro Street address, was a great and beautiful island like the description of Prince Edward Island. However, like the island of Atlantis, my dreams of investment there sank into an impious security.

In another world of realization, Brian, also King of legend, was reputed to have obtained kinship of all of Ireland with the help of the Danes. The reality of my family bible to the daughter of Brian also made this a threat to the illiterate classes of literature to home-based schooling. Here is where I divided the language of literature with the language of colour. I was the artist and my husband was the poet for the professional treatise. Like the Precambrian Shield's Melville Monument though, I was hurled out onto a monolith far greater than any WWI monument in our domain created to honour the service of war heroes.

I recommended to myself the work of Simon Schama's "Landscape and Memory" to console my connection between the esoteric and the reality of a newspaper article written about a vehicle accident which took place in Summerside at an address which accuses all drivers at fault. Here is where my only daughter was proof to a false accusation since it begins with a false premise. My logistical analysis was not always financially mathematical since just because all dogs are animals, it does not mean that all animals are dogs. The modern researcher instructs, "You are never allowed to speak as though you are a representative of a group just because you are a paid employee." The dead will not suffer the ecumenical debate! Yet the President will have cause to judge the living and to entrap the female counterpart to the marriage of the lamb through the schism of Adam and Eve with their relationship to God.

I reread the article of my Defence of Military Merit. The Reverend certainly had a morbid sense of humor to dictate the certificate falsely. As I approached Janus, the Roman God of doors, the sir name Muise was reconstituted to my memory moving forward to the name of William and the "Chronicles of Narnia" to my educated children. The supply of these literatures was different than the encyclopedias of my childhood and they were capitalistic to the world of children. So now I wait in solitude for what is really expected to be presented with these two orphans with an actual event verses the physical experience of proof to war or peace on the treatise of government statistics understanding the messages across Asgard.

Janus was a god of beginnings, doors and gates, time, duality, passages and endings. From architecture, it did not mean that one could conquer the world with these two faces though. One represented the future and the other represented the past. The uniqueness of obtaining a place in history was not unlike any other character created for parenthetical thought and the culture of the time of empire builders has left us shorthanded in the realm of ownership to the truth. In the democracy of the heredic avenue from the beginning of an ensign, there were revolving doors in the modern world of commerce. Thus, the etymological list of civilizations which began with the book of Genesis followers were not of the same elk as those of the Cambrian House of my Nova Scotia homeland. The Akkad, a onetime city in ancient Babylon, gave an accounting emergency to the poets of Italian currency. From this presentation to the coup between two worlds of Roman Britons with those of Norman Britons was the Brian of a financial foe in pursuit of the Emerald Island for himself. He would attempt this with the aid of the Grant of Probate Courts.

Geologists are very detailed in the calculation of natural resources. Any attempt at an exorcism on behalf of the land title is classified as inappropriate behavior. The members of the Coptic Church of the ancient Egyptian Empire was also inappropriate as its doctrine in practice was considered condemned by the Council of Chalcedon. Today, the Council of Bryan, is also considered inappropriate to the home ownership of the female author as artist and not poet even though she has won merit as such for the literary award. I have read enough Canadian literature to realize the Ghoul attached to the sir name of a Western Mennonite by tenure of Queen's University to those of the Military College with the nickname of Komi to the Anna Karenina book of Leo Tolstoy suddenly appearing on the floor at the same time we linked the team's name with those of the Commissars. The harm caused by the intents of D.H. Lawrence by our own Canadian born Alistair Macleod were all along the same shelf in the bookcase.

The lessons learned within their texts were not visible over the many hours it took to repair the house into a livable working space for the artist. They were also not detached to the security of English Ireland as opposed to Catholic Iowa. However the people listed here in social insurance numbers to the military profession of ownerships of copyright are real threats to the matched security of communications names such as Mickey, Melvin and Dunlop especially when it comes to the origin of natural law and the post-de-la-Belaine factors of the degree of reason. As part of the assurance of the mother, I will safely reply to the auditors of my household and the obelisk, both were designed to ward away death.

Generally, I didn't or ever had a mind for entertaining the occult. On the one hand there was the Peach and on the other hand there was a penguin of publishers' addresses. Same old, dam old. Could we afford to protect the copyright of Athena over the copyright of Minerva? Yet this same situation of mystical events did not satisfy the complete action to protect oneself in the face of systematic death. I am not referring to the difference between a chain letter and that of an association plot within the security of sabotage. We are talking about the systematic destruction of taxpayers to their rights of ownership to their land because of not being capable of differentiating the employment of the owner to the owner of the unemployed in society. Here is where Lenfesky had departed from Keynes.

Thankfully the science of biology was introduced to both our children at just the right time where Armida was not the character viewed as being inappropriate to the liturgy. Otherwise stated, Jerusalem delivered was not relevant to the Canadian Gazette. In this way what was enlisted to showcase instead were the beaches of Cavendish where the aeolian dune deposits against a scarped surface in Prince Edward Island prepared the visual reality between the old and new in a balance of peaceful retreats. In other words-the vacation of scarce resources.

Luckily also, understanding the crusades in their language was not as interesting to the history of the participation in NATO exercises after the Cold War. We did although, want the Russians to understand our inclusions as alumni to the Federal Government's policy of believing in our academic study over the avowed vocational institutions. We became aware, as latecomers in the province of Ontario, to the dangers lurking at the crossing of the political borders. Abet I have a much better understanding of the political elite in Canada's first capital city where she will carry on with her sibilant into the future.

I had no power to stop those intents of instruction. They began with the publications of the Queen's Journal. The whisper of articulation with rude deliverance of an email from the sir name Cohrs where I have also witnessed the sign of Mary Cohrs on the Air Canada hockey arena of investment in Toronto. My best local accusation to the intrusion was that it was an honourary architect who summoned the communication to the value chain.

Chain letters are allotment forms of threats and are classified as illegal in Canada. Crosby, from the same province as my children, is a Canadian icon to the hockey league and to the equally recognizable Don Cherry. The name Sid thou, historically referenced, was a Spanish champion of Christianity in the eleventh century where a poem idealized him figuratively as an hero. In export development circles, farm credit corporations are normally lower or on par with government stocks. Maybe that phone call from Joan, from those exports of military personnel, could have initiated the Rockwood institution after the troops were returning to their lots from a tour in Afghanistan. I generally feared however, that it also induced the Raymond clan to sabotage my canopy presentation which was financially and legally a registered business appropriately measured for a Canadian dollar amount. It could have very easily have represented both the account with the money supply. The gallery knew the name Pimm as referencing the skew to a distilled whiskey in the Ontario Liquor Control Board where she was the bar staff to tenured commerce PhDs. The distribution of those brand names also contracts inside every province in Canada. Therefore, we had to begin the journey of report against the slander of legal correspondence of visible tender to the invisible troops that were retired and existed to entrap an individual patron. It was obvious that the accounting function for both the legal and administrative function departments of career managers did not border on the truth.

WHIMIS is a self-study program just like the PIP is for nuclear, chemical and biological warfare. An editor for the local newspaper takes the job as associate professor for the military college and the Reverend gets away with the commission of selling our family out of our home. I personally would not see job losses just to apportion the debt on to our children as a means of scare tactics. To have a vehicle written off from a cosmetic fault at the expense of the female driver is as unforgivable as the push off the sidewalk was to my Anabaptism.

Among the Senate, we have sent a willful understanding for the I as in I am alive, and we are not as dumb as you think I look. I also am the elected member to the writings submitted on behalf of the Ministry of Education in Ontario to my attached DF & E which I paid for, not my spouse. The architect knowingly sent my renderings out to the cult leader of the 411 College Street detail without realizing he was being unethical in that process without consulting the ownership principle. This would be true for both official languages. A walk down the deserted Rue Charest Est in the old city of Quebec shows the meddlesome insurance claim of the Citadel to hire its guards. It is just too bad there are so many enemies today as there were in the years prior to 1867.

It took her twenty-five years to replace the couch that the Norman broke. Likewise, it took an eternity of titles to finally point to the Janus of the Roman God here at the gallery.

As master to the certificate of mangers, at least architecturally in metric, the specifications are perfect according to the professional status of residential neighborhoods. The renderings are workable to the honest broker. Be forewarned however, of the Russian mafia to take back the amber traffic light to access and censure material against your only son.

The Birth of an Angel

Returning to the Spirit from Silent Hands
Written for my mother with reference
to the license AD 405

What type of words would you have
for a mother's departing spirit,
except that the cold snow
feels good on one's tear stained face.
I feel trees passing by the windows of this train,
moils of vibrating tendrils:
All sorts of servers offering their trust;
tenets willingly offered
to care for the tarnished image upon his brow.

I am horrified by this call to arms
that has me painfully
clinging past crystals of ice
forming eyelets in the passionless air.
There is no violence to belie, yet every imperfection
adorns this cruise along a wintery sky.
Below there is the shadow of a daybreak,
the chatter of starving birches
displaying their spidery webs
beside tall firs of black augers.
Bogs are there in the mind
that hunt a nation's stride,
tensile now for the soul whose thoughts are fled.
Her vigil stands for the ones
who gambled with our lives

and lost. She also weeps and hopes
for something best known
that her forest child could send.

There is a statue called
Our Lady of the Saguenay River where a marine fjord
meets the St. Lawrence River Established in 1988.

Most Christians believe that angels have always been here with us people on earth unlike Shiva and Kali. However, it has only recently been shown how that could never have been the case in the trilogy of God verses man. It might also be important to remind myself that I have never really sought out the spiritual gifts that religious men cling to on behalf of the humanities. I see their effigies as I see the lady of the Saguenay River. They are not real, just associates following documentation, tapping out the farms and communities which dared us to be mature parents, to season and blossom as a species of divided construction following our own subgroups.

I think and believe the facts and I have read that there are many levels of accountability from the knowledge of the first window to be broken by a baseball. Thus, today I do believe in angels and if it were not for the formal introduction of a geographical term with its applicable resources, that we are available to build upon the earth. For example, the word "subdivision" means the same biologically as it does for practical building code purposes. The National Audubon Society sites and I paraphrase so as not to get into any trouble with publishing rights, casual and informal descriptions such as race, phase, form and variation. Then descriptions are subdivided into more technical data such as height, flower, habitat, range and additional comments. On the other hand, Joe, the plumber is not anybody of significance until the infrastructure of a model community starts to advance itself into a sterile span of building codes and life spans of known building materials. If insured, it wouldn't matter if Joe lived in Tokyo or Baffin Island. The familiarity of the need for services to emergency situations allows all people to move from one common point on the planet to another with relative safety.

As for the destruction of the person, this should never happen and if it does then we would have a need to call on an Angel. Today it would still be classified as an act of respect for the person who is wrongfully convicted as far as customary respects go. The window is also a building detail that is a customary respect for the canting arm. It means pure light, wisdom and piety that are attributes of great people. Thus, as an artist, I believe that the reflection is not a mirror to letting the paint itself become the shadow as texture to the filter work that the camera does for photography to show that, like Samson, there are immortal aspects of our conscience.

A jihad never changes so be careful who you vote for if remaining true to your culture. On the day of voting, I will not be afraid. Remember that X=lock, r=red and k=cat. They are asymmetries as they are incomplete forms of information. Like engineers, they are very risky information systems to employ. Unless you must believe in mythical or abstract number systems, then don't go exchanging Ogopogo for a Phoenix. This is how I would enforce an influential treaty on behalf of a distinguished person. A treaty means unquestionable belief. A philosophical treaty means you must unquestionably believe in God. Politics has never ever done that. An army therefore will always train for war. I left.

Some things are not forgivable to the management of people and resources and this type of Government is outside my priority to safety and navigation. Furthermore, the egg must always be protected. If your spouse is missing in the legal sense, then God help you as a taxpayer. I hoped that these stories could be read and understood. On behalf of the people, I arranged a beginning entry. It was my way to ensure more democratic commissions. Federalism is not an heritage route or a cairn. The obelisk has a purpose in writing. There are none in these covers though. So, the book will protect your property and your obligations to office. Remain committed to your country, not the campaign. Poems appreciate life in the expressive faculty of management services. I certainly hoped she liked mine. I gave my best words for her peace. There was the intent to identify with the land.

The rocks are balanced perfectly, then permanently fixed into place with a visionary testament. It is more than just a simple piece of art. They stand, encourage us and they travel with us. I have found many rare trees and shrubs growing in these same soils on various properties. Their grounds are level with mounds of barren places, all very different from the hanging pots and walls of babies' breath and English Ivy. In fact they are almost like a prebendary oath, an extension of spiritual prosperity; not administration.

Quebec is always in a state of contempt for courts. The Great Seal of Canada is our hopeful remedy. For me it seemed my hands must have been cleaned in order to become an ancestral leader. Its Inukshuk though may not have been mobile enough for today's industry measure of dry goods. It seemed to me now only like some isometric painting with a new listing. We knew what it was missing in the ensign, yet the Golden eagle flew with her office.

The miracle was in the academics of repositioning maps. Some were dogwoods. Others were slang versions of female personifications. A sailor is not a sailor when he is not at sea. The head is tactfully more than just a state. She is not a social belligerent. Her mission is absolute. She is a remedy, not the molarity with expertise.

The Princess Royal was a visitor to our community of military personnel. Peter and Zara were born consecutively in 1977 and 1981. My children were only fifteen months apart and yet these two children concern me for our own safety. Science defines the quart as one twentyfourth of the Gibraltar coin. That is a stable equation. It rests beyond the realm of original sin and it is a global concept. Vote for whoever you want, just don't forget to secure a living for yourself. Pay yourself first for you are possible and a presence if in need of an Angel.

Christianity was not a passing grade to the test of time or education. For any group of people, the publicity is to negotiate peace and prosperity enough to remain invested. The new international version had changed the dress codes and therefore there was no connection to the congregation of monarchical titles. That is why the canting arm of the College was so important according to the Great Seal and the interpretations of Canadian Law. We are not primates. Wages had to be paid and governments were to make sure the underground economy did not mar its specific performance. See order 19 to Avens, meaning, "On the strength of your own merit." For the William Faulkner, it challenges an antithesis in Art.

Today I realize the 911 system of exchanges are not going to help the North American markets. The womanizers of the leadership campaigns built the exclusion factor into the system and every system that use any link to that one model of a man will vice the conduct for all.

We had to think outside the box. That would be the only strategy to employ. The name William was the media source material that we needed in order to secure the future of Canada. It could not be a trademark and art is still a virtue worth owning. Besides, my children could not be bound by acts of indecency which took place before they were born.

Flap Jacks are like Fly Tippers. The RCMP were trumped by the President of the United States. Criminals really did have the Upper Canadian franchise surrounded and they probably even had enough clout to take over the CRA in the global economy. Since there is a link between the unwed mother and the teacher, money or the scarcity of it made the emblem a counterfeit issue since unlike money which is divisible, portable, stable and not easy to counterfeit by the majority of our population, the weak link had to be the maple leaf which was used by every illegal team of immigrations' lawyers to their advantage on the markets of exchange to international suasion powers. The parallel between money and art is indiscreet. The law and its lawyers are not so stable.

Military campaigns needed money and resources. The unfortunate dilemma is that there is no return on your investment as soon as the uniform becomes soiled by the smearing comments of media sources. Money has no heart. It does only one thing. It provides a medium of exchange for the satisfaction of a temporary emotional gain. It was the job of government to ensure the Minister of Income provided an equal rate of pay to close the gap between gender inequality. It also forgot to set the standard from where those employees come from. If I am being eliminated from a modern high rise construction due to the fact that the crane operation can manage to retain his seat without having to empty his bladder, then the inequality of jobs is not the issue, it is the biological elimination by one person on the job site. Today immigration has increased to the point that superpower countries are creating so much stress on the middle class that the return to gnostic couples and the esoteric conversion of decent loving families is a drogue in our returning office.

Our departments of National Defence are indeed in an economic crisis. Falsifying legal baptismal certificates relating to the mother of her own children is just one example. Once the ceremony is over, that is when you see the entrapment. There are others, I fear, who have been equally vexed. Our situation is still ongoing within the Courts. Compulsory military service engages the act of taking someone else's life as your own. In our engagement, this could not happen since both parents are belonging to the crown. Yet the tour through the Musee des Beaux Arts on the 400th anniversary of the city of Quebec, brought the taxation of heavy artillery to bear down on the elimination of women to their career promotions. All we could do was protect our property by the courage of conviction.

In the domain of medical fact, women cannot order breast milk from the hospital dispensary. Thus, the service of a kab, as derived of the meaning of the smallest measure of dry goods, is a more stable measurement than those of a mole of substance. Since the earth contains samples of uranium, gold or even just conglomerates of crystals, there is no secret to the intelligence of opting out of an organization which seeks to trap the language of the mother tongue in a democratic vote.

I realized the abuse to women outside the country's jurisdictions. Canadian were sent to Afghanistan to provide services of health in dentistry, hygiene and policing. The resources it took to gather the population against the threat of death has been a form of reverse psychology to many Canadians of past military campaigns. It took fourteen years of research into the diversity of our topography and our political history to see this crisis for what its effects would be in the investment of our businesses and the ownership of property against a communist state. Gal is an abbreviated form for liquid measure which refers to approximately four quarts in whatever units one chooses to source for the containment of that product to market. Since oil paint is a combination of kabs and gals in exact recipes of measurements, then the business of employing those materials justifies the markets to be open for business.

"I will deliver out of the hand of the wicked and I will redeem out of the hand of the terrible." This is an example of something we want to avoid in business. In 2001 we were reinstated from the family names of origin. The crisis was not a hoax. The reason for my bewilderment rested with the sanitary napkin deposited in my mailbox to which the electronic algorithm to produce paper products for distribution was a premeditated insult to my intelligence. I also take great umbrage in the authority of the Ministry of Health to spend scarce resources on such a campaign during the crisis in Haiti. Even my name was correctly spelled which was a first since my husband and I were married. The name Robert was decimated as a result of this evolution in marketing to present the most vulgar and contemptuous presentation to my household. We are not cats dropping off mice to offer their owners and the act was very debatable as to who initiated the campaign and why were the costs approved for this by our Ministry of Health. I personally would have had more common sense for gender neutrality forms of stolid grounds in education than this type of liberal agenda. We have earned the gallery of officers to select a better grade of leadership.

I wrote a song for the people of Haiti. In fact, it was a lullaby; possibly thinking in hindsight of the word Abegweit, meaning cradled on the waves. The refrain does not have any really defined musical notation. Its harmony just seems to go on like the tides and there is no version that can ever be made more correct than the other. I've designed its poetry to be just that way. Someday when you see it written, you too may see the tangibility of music which has seen rocks deposited by glaciers older than our generations of political prowess or incorporation of city states. Nobody can predict the future, however in order to save, one must be willing to take the test. Armida created a little space for me personally to create a garden. To me it represents life with a gold amulet. I must be alive to appreciate its design.

CHAPTER TWO

FROM NO PIGS TO COWS

If you were born in 1984, it would be good advice to take some Spanish lessons. Passover ended on Sir William Edmond Logan's birthday the year they flew over the Rocky Mountains. I was gifted with the overall surprise of paying for that field course. Now it is all just water under the bridge to our island province and I am the soldier who doesn't get to wear bullet proof vests.

The apartment was furnished in standard fashion. Nothing too expensive and nothing too grandiose. I sensed the air of Italian suspicion as we were let into the schematics of the bedroom. As the men drank to their chamber of commerce that night, the obsession with the shock of the Chipin to the chemistry of their Bishop must have seen that the person was not having any fun with the sport of curling anymore. Thus, as the snow fell, I took the legal entitlement to the name to speak on behalf of the ethics to the sport with the art of the OEM.

This city was huge, and its legacy was just as looming. However, I was not there to lobby the roses of the graduation ceremony into hard times. Charles had already accomplished that leadership. The gift was the covering to a watercolour with the protocol of light fading away as fiction to a stanchion of glass for white wine. Again, I question the minds of people to market this token for accomplishment just like I questioned the sanitary napkin.

The poem of exile began with Esa. It was his own punishment for having divided the syllables in such a way as to remove the daughter from the formal coda. The epilogue begins with the walking through the citadels of our dear homeland. "Grant that you walk a free soul with the lessons learned as streams of fame: fallow the bow to the realm of established works to claim."

Her daughter grew up to be beautiful and famed for the things the eye could see who measured the duty of the sea of every region to honour their names. The first they sought for themselves. The architecture was famous as were the Elizabethan houses where the whole occupancy was a gallery of Hanovers. Spitalfields were a London altar outside of this diocese. It was a different form of classical literature where this new Prince Regent was forming the clientele of elegant sculpture.

His street designs, both upper and lower Canadian, were departures from the alleys of mazes where landscapers now hid functional utilities. The photograph is toward the east. Here for a moment they sat on the shores across from the Island's airport to observe the flights of aviators. It was then that she realized her house would not be a brick box of domestic America. It would be open, airy and strong like the timberline of the Appalachians. It would be attributed to the classical simplicity of charm, light and a d'esprit des patron du Canada. It would be a boarding house with all the amenities for the gallery ascots and finally it would recreate where the old fort had dismantled.

While reorganizing the research material for its completion, the hamlet of this painting template was fooled by the municipality of Doug Gilmore charitable vehicle enterprises. The vehicle accident linked the visual with the spiritual in such a way as to pressure the Noel sir name in the proof of the province of Ontario to the first born of family names.

The Genesis derivation and Exeter now engaged in the financial system to the statistics of a death rate to the Norman airport. The inhabitants of the White City, the Rose of Osim, went directly to the proof of Ariel Sharon. It was a rudder to provide military law and English contract law. I was the one with enough experience to suggest the death rate is just as important as the accident rate either of transportation or of childbirth. Here Peddle is a sir name just as Fairchild is to the communications museum. The informant was relating the fact that Newfoundland was a fact of the Canadian Forces of the Ottawa archival yellow records to business associations and non-profit Legion memberships. However, Debbie, married a US Marine. Her Lawrence name is now a Mississippi or Missouri attachment along interstate addresses of homes below the Canadian Border Services Agency. Her father's final words were delivered to the public as, "Why didn't they put her on the pill?"

This is what it is like to be hurt in a way that will never be righted. The dirty deed had been accomplished with the absolute armament to the perfect crime in reverse psychology. The science of protection not really a protection at all and it was indeed her antithesis: man.

On her own property, she could see the natural path of light like that which enters the diamond cutter's tools: the shinning waters of her beloved Prince Edward as the sun passes through the clouds. At sunset the blues, greys and purples shift into a crimson oasis of meadow weeds in contrast to the blacked teeth of the mouth which delivered the oral tradition. In contrast to the winged sculpture of salutes to her day of colour in peace at her feet from the lamplight of perfect days, was the sorrow to bear witness to this truth.

The history of the falls as I was attending classes for the ex officio of my career was the Niagara region. I always read a book of motivation before I take to the canvas. The book chosen was the published version by Pierre Burton and thus began the painting titled Measurement. As for Paul Johnson who wrote dedicating his book to the memory of Hugh Fraser, was added to it with the report:

Israeli Prime Minister Benjamin Netanyahu, right, stands with Foreign Minister Ariel Sharon, center, during a one-minute silent tribute to the 34,000 Jews killed by the Germans in 1941 in Babi Yar, Ukraine, yesterday. Netanyahu came on a one-day visit to Discuss peace efforts in the Middle East and economic and trade questions with Ukraine's President, Leonid Kuchma. A security guard is on the left, others are unidentified.

The reading of this article and the book to the words of my own biological flesh and blood was indeed a red-letter day. The Associated Press takes credit for the photograph were the Adidas Logo distinctly separates the identified with the unidentified. At that moment in time, the printed death notice of my own mother was delivered by my spouse as he arrived home with the message. Her passing and the deliberate omission of me to receive the next of kin notification meant that my own sister had gone out of her way to make the schism continue into my marriage using the Government of Canada archives to my military career seem very criminally intended.

This was of course far from the truth and the Veritas Vincit became the alibi to prove this was an entrapment and so the vestments changed hands yet again.

The experiment to the true ownership to the family bible was corrected with the Bibles purchased from the Jewish community in Toronto. If ever there needed to be a peace between two siblings, it would be accomplished from the pages of this book. I returned the book written by a neighbor Clinton Morrison, Jr. to my father. The memory for me was the poem I wrote to ensure her peace from the photo taken while on route to her dedication ceremony with my daughter to ensure perfect peace. Little did I know that this too would come back to haunt me after my father's death in 2017 by the courts of Probate and Donald I. Schurman.

The Indian in the cupboard continued with the military security over my accommodation since 1979 to the address 18 Breadlebane, PE. Now there will always be two places in Canada which I will never return. This means that systematically, the revenue generated from my life either professionally or socially, will never include NL and Toronto. As the associate committee on national building codes show the administration without a means of liquid refreshment of celebration for her day of birth and the captain of every month who is not an all male organization, the land, as a personal parcel in the jurisdiction of authority to currency preference shows the ownership absolutely and to the mindfulness of her good works. I am not dead.

Psalms sound like palms if you were I and considering the amount of paperwork used to prove her innocence of purpose to the regime of Sikhs in Canada and for any vehicle past or future in all commands from coast to coast was as intended in the memory of lands she called her own. So, don't go judging me by your own thoughts or actions D.H. If I must take aim to protect the actions of one, I have been legally trained to take action for all. In the report on the foster parent, the girl died after the CAS (Children's Aid Society) tried to infiltrate with a girl by the name of Sierra, also a GMC motor company brand name. Not much wonder why the Cavalier was written off by the insurance adjuster on behalf of the female military trained professional operator. The entrapment was to the mother of Shinea, the sister of Sierra, as she is convicted of murder. She was then sent to a women's criminal institution in Kingston, Ontario.

As for the Ottawa archives to the ownership of names to my siblings, was the copyright to this publication purchased from my own registrations of ownership to land and capital, that was not part of the NHL Gilmour enterprises or Dory and Tolgyesi brokers but is the Abegweit Flight Path. It is not a logo. It is a proof of a flight path and the belief in the reason for that flight path in the forward thinking of family situations against a criminal mind as opposed to a military mind is the presence of peace. The copyright, if in doubt by the employees of accounting to taxation, to the truth should not be preoccupied with the religious belief of extracting a confession which would be of no consequence to anyone.

As a professional, I think that the fact of expropriation and exploitation is not really the issue here. It is the destruction of a human soul in much the same way that the Germans did in 1941. Furthermore, the solicitation by the foster parent community may be guilty of trying to secure a Presidency here in Canada.

Slander and smeer campaigns are criminally intended by local political populations. However, their standards are always reporting to somebody and that somebody may be entering illegally into the public account of records. My daughter's copyright was used with permission even though no copyright existed between them internationally. Art is always an international story. Cartoon characters are not. If discussing my career with my son by the name of William Barker, do you not think that the name Baum would not be of concern to a maiden name? The Smith of the Book of Mormon is a bane to our employment existence and for that reason I acted appropriately when the real authority of the law was absent or corrupt as shown by this story I am revealing.

A person whose first name is Francis made a statement of not being capable of reading a book. Does this also mean that they would not be capable of writing one either? If you belong to an administration outside of Canadian Law, then the premise of misleading a Canadian taxpayer should be punishable by law. My veritas vincit in Latin was not meant for the pigs. I also do not work for the badge with the "Jimmy" on it. My spouse knew what type of jealousy he was inflicting on her when he came home with the news of her mother's death. I did not take the oath in order to entrap individuals into accepting work without pay, as in a gulag situation. That is exactly what I am suggesting is willful blindness by police forces to her ownership and peaceful existence.

Elements to Negative GMT

Elements are only one stable size Melted
flakes, gasped in sometimes.
Fiery Lords, streams and lakes,
Fantasies, dreams, myths to create.
All are swords in liquid motion. Feathered birds
cupped in hand, Offering haste, securely faced:
Little ones inane as clay.
Majestically their day rises
Vigilantly suffering friend to foe.
Woven scarfs, bare on parchment:
Nature's reason, thunder opposes.

I once held a tiny bird in my hand.
Rejoicing in the strength of his wiry
feet, I was lifted up into his sky.

Rogers' first name is attached to the clinical vasectomy. At the heart of this story is the financial obligation of this person to the military campaign. It is not a factor of my being a mother. Yet it does have consequences for the religious iconography and the Pope. Similarly, the EA to the Mayor's office is using the seasoning of Rosemary to the vexation of all taxpayers to try to maintain order against the derogatory name of Warford for the descendants of Africa. It wasn't I who said she was bumptious. If in the selection of a degree, it might be obvious to mention what it means to mention the Cree politician by the name of Mathew.

With that name we have a whole host of debates attached to the hiring of the next issue of writers for Quebec's sovereignty where hydroelectric megaprojects gather personal weapons for co-parenting perfidious, renewing language demonstrations. All these actions of unsolicited marketing have been challenging my autonomy for over twenty-two years beginning with the name Allison-Burra from her appointment when my children were without a social insurance number.

So, when it comes to the industrial design of the building itself, know for sure that it is something I would never approve for sellable purposes. If you believe that the law acts to protect everyone equally, then why would the political elite in this city enforce an obligation to a decree which is clearly so controversial that many people would instantly reject. Since I acted as an individual, then the federalists had a better chance to entrap that same individual. This shifts the vital link between rural logistics transportation specialization with enforceable standing order contracts to put police in their boots as auditors of the general political summons of innocent taxpayers. Judging by the amount of retail businesses, the coppersmiths of contra flow electricity to the board of civil aviation authorities are a Coptic church of holes. Here is where the record of what I am saying becomes like a structure of Administration. The first names of those two children are Benjamin with an obelisk and Shinea with the same obelisk. Hope for Mr.

L.W. Oakly, the assignment for the resentment on behalf of the Crown of Whig Standards has complied with section 20 of the Canadian Part 1 Electrical Codes which deals with flammable liquids dispensing and service stations, garages, bulk storage plants, finishing processes and aircraft hangers.

Since it is a fact of existence that Canada's building codes do not cover surveillance towers or aerial towers such as radio or microwave, it may signal the inverse relationship between Coast Guard employees and military frigates to recruit into nothingness especially if you are a female and the CPP benefits would not be available to you since it is a Liberal strategy in the end game.

The venomous attack at my ownership privilege to vehicle ownership was a personal attack on the capitalistic account of manufacturers to the Provinces. The mules were not of Darwinian design, they were part of the Command for the Squadron of pilots. Again, it is stated that slander is a chargeable offence. My qualifications are as valid today as they were in 1995. And since I am the post-Confederate author of "Abscission" where the Belaine meets the medical ghost ship to the Townsend of Cape Breton rims, the Silhouette 1767 graphic art image is what I have established for the whispers of Joshua, Sophie, Miller and Wade.

Take highway 15 to Lyndhurst. Turn right on Lyndhurst Road. Before reaching Lyndhurst, turn right, just before the Home Hardware on Highway 3. Continue driving for 3-5 minutes past the yellow house on the left, over the bridge. After the bridge turn right, following the sign to Shawmere. You are now on a side road. Follow turn on mailbox signs to Shawmere until you reach a house and fishing cabins.

This is something that you will not destroy in order to make me look like an idiot just wandering around on the highway.

The curtain call for that week on stage revealed the following scene by the small theatre company. Two white Caucasians are found in a public bathroom. Both are naked. The more prominent image is kneeling with the body's first half hidden inside the toilet bowl revealing his buttocks to the audience. The second image is balanced along the back wall revealing the feminine physique as if knowing that rigor mortis would set in after the act was complete.

CHAPTER THREE

CAN JOT

The sales lady passed the receipt to me." Do you want this in the bag, or do you want to keep it with you?"

I took it and put it in the bag, and we left the store satisfied with the purchase transaction.

Wendover is a city in Utah State. Witchcraft is still practiced in Salem; MA and I am the Chairperson tasked with picking up the last remains of a salvage aircraft for the CSIS investigation team that followed its return to Canada.

I resent the subscribed wishes of the people in both states. As an artifact of the lone ace journey was the encryption of my national emblem as an earned credit without the uniform to back me up. I doubt very much that any student would have been capable of making this nine-day journey to barter their entry into the varsity sports of University training.

I began the painting before she even knew what my occupation title was. Someday it may well be known. Since I have accessed copyright law, I will not rename my children no matter what number is assigned to them for employment ROEs. My words are written to be maintained by the eyes and minds of trained professionals. My badge of honour placed this year to commemorate the erythrocytic poppy on my grandfather's behalf. It was an opportunity again to rest the ghosts of the epitaphs' epaulets since my father-in-law is death too.

I have an ephah of the kitchen since the man Mr. L. Cole prejudiced my military performance to suggest a miscarriage. From the bunker in that isolated posting nobody would have believed me anyway. Moving forward to the Pollock of 155 Greenlees Drive and the attachment of names to military titles, was the Jan to the first-born male in the lineage of user manuals of the many vehicle registrations in the CFB quarterly reports. This is where the term "Title Skipping" is a proof to the entrapment of jotting down this dairy discussing how the privilege of the male lineage is not a discredit to the family name, yet those of the Eve pattern of sexual femininity is classified as a form of disease carrying mosquito. Disraeli and Rosen would be discussing how honour and personal feelings can sometimes depress the economy and nepotism in royalty is carefully watching the Olympic equestrian results. To this end the Chamber of Commerce to her works of art were paid in full for their commercial account.

In the account of designing living spaces within the law, it is solely for the protection of the innocent where the building materials have proven a successful function with an inspiring endorsement to an attractive permanent candidate of the feminine gender as well.

So, when I went back to look at that receipt at the end of the year you can imagine my shock. There was, from the till, a receipt produced which showed a date that could never have existed in my life time or yours and I wondered why it was that the issue of such a receipt could have gone unnoticed by so many people in the local business district. The auditor would have missed this account, being only concerned with the odometer reading of the vehicles entered for the data bases of the Ministry of Transportation to her Dr. Richardson. So how could we address this reconciliation with the Ministry of Commerce when in fact I have no idea how it was programmed into their cash register to begin with? She made the point of capturing my attention when she asked whether I wanted the receipt in the bag or not.

The regulations in the military are exhaustive, yet they are not illegal. Sometimes a lullaby helps us get through the phenomena either off or on crown land. One cannot be penalized for doing their job and where the sanity of one is the sanity for all, I have realized that the world of commerce does not come with a set of rules or regulations attached. In this tiny shop of yarn where the immortal space was accomplished, it transformed the liberty of ownership to a receipt with a different level of training exercise. Once she claimed the receipt, there was no time to argue the amount of investment into her occupation.

Within the law, there is no honour among thieves. I tried every combination of day, month and year only to conclude that there never was such a day recorded in North America. If conducting the point of purchase sale intention, I thought to myself, "Please don't steal into the hearts of the innocent even if they are only just soldiers to boot." So, remember to tell the truth in the event of attempted empowerment of others and then walk away completely from the situation. The finer layers of risk are always dignified. Just learn to develop the subject matter, maintain that you will always sing better than the dead and then build the structure according to the living attributes with light as breathable as fresh air.

Our legacy could never be Moslem. At the time of her convocation, the Premier was Rodney MacDonald. Her application was always a lottery as to whether she would return the next year. When an education system challenges the employment based on gender this way, a sinister recovery from the grievance to the year of our postings was what the Province of Ontario Attorney Generals used to collect their sir names for the army vehicles of the Toronto regiments. Financially, the office shows just how jealous one person can be when deprived of their livelihood under the conditions of a Liberal occupational analysis to the marriage of both Masters.

In lighthouses we know and understand protection. Yet in the occupation of an institution, whose canopy do you sleep under at night? In order to answer this question, I investigated the cartoon version of "Alice in Wonderland" where the characters Tweedle Dee and Tweedle Dum are depicted as twins. So now let's enter into the liturgy of the discussion of why somebody would get involved with the Foster Parent's Plan when you already have a beautiful family of your own without the twins to mess around with the time analysis of the owners to the title of Government offices. Realizing that all names are combinations of letters: we use twenty-six which can be either capital or lower case. As for the taxation of land holdings, the military having federal jurisdiction, allowed this family to be free of any amount of yearly taxation either for police, schools, roads or employment, to instead be a service to mediate the marriage of adoption and forced communal housing verses our taxes paid to home ownership principles and academic titles of Masters instead of Ms.

The motivation of economic theory meant that at the end of the day, somebody would have ownership. In the case of Wendy, nobody has ownership of anything and like the receipt of a date which could not exist, the citizens themselves had to learn to walk away from the situation. In order to accomplish this however, I kept a journal of abbreviations. B is the letter in all Bachelor programs invested at Canadian Universities where education has an interest to a party of associations and clubs. It was within that experience that I have found the letters B.Q. which is Latin for Bene Quiescat or Rest in Peace. Now while the alumni made their networks of scalpers for the provinces of Ontario and Quebec, the taxation of other provinces and their social insurance numbers were being eroded by the belief that some people were living without a conscience while some of us were paying double the taxes and still working twenty-four seven for the titles worn in the Administration of Canada. I gave my address for the D-Day address on behalf of my maiden name. The logo still is not attached to the CGEP program of the Dupuis year of birth where the I.C.E. is the Institute of Civil Engineers.

The D.R. of the Wendy association to business in the Toronto GTA realized that death was following his research into the Afghanistan war. Here they used the widowing formula as a valuable lesson when it came to the hard line of Catholic Priests on the historic governance of legal tender. Therefore, it was part of my obligation to my children to find out why it was that my occupational code and titles were omitted from the archives of military records along with the birth dates of my children.

The encomium research read was the d.v.p. meaning decessit vita patris which means that his son certifiably died in his father's lifetime for which my C.M. was a certified Master. Although not a master of surgery, the L.A. version of the title was still accountable for the person literate in Arts from which my lessons taught were still probably considered more protecting than my own father when viewing the M.C. of the Military Cross Mother recipients against the still born seal of the ill-fated Newfoundland Regiment. I gave them both titles: "Devil's Island and Cape Bloomington and Cape Split." Both were interpretations of Canadian landscapes where the M.I.5 moles remonstrate every branch of military intelligence dealing with security and the reality of life. The motivation to the M5 code was the finalization to the followers and believers of the Shakespearian tragedy as an alla which forced one act to either kill or be killed by another act like the characters of the famed poem Beowulf. As the Doctor on the Board of Education, these dialogues would have been an easy assumption to make on behalf of the Liberal agenda to the financial burden of mother over the father.

Did he have to kill her? That is the question to jot down. I mean if the characters were a reported faculty, would they have the power to change the gender of Tweedle Dee and Tweedle Dum and would greater respect or disgrace be attributed to them?

If I am forced to respect the titled tenure, then should they not also respect the ensign for which we found our country to be relied upon for its own safety and security to an absolute dollar amount instead of the weight of an unjust system in society? That is why ownership was to be respected and the copyright whether you like or dislike the material and effort to complete its registration. The titles are absolute. Nobody can change this in my lifetime and the genetics of the science of two sets of twins in caricature may be someway linked to the motivation of the economics in human action. A5 was meant to mean (or mien) to keep your law books close at hand if one equates the motivational impulse to drink alcohol as the same motivational impellent used by commerce to declare a welcome to all sexually motivated individuals on behalf of all residents.

Where there are widows and widowers, the explicit presentation of Elaine pining away could also mean the lettered individual a threat to bear witness in the event of another d.v.p. The dictionary differentiated the gender to be specific in terms of a widow over the widower and the first name Elaine was a correspondent to both books of Samuel. One was given my B.Q. with the Doctor as witness to the peace offered. The other was given in trust to my Remembrance Day event message for the accident of proof to the province of Prince Edward Island. The social life of the occupancy of houses means the ones in which she owns and pays taxes for. In 2010, the author of "The Forgiven Soldier" was for herself in what she had to do in order to right the things that went wrong that were not her fault. Yet, because of other misunderstandings of their services of utilities providers from one province to another, there were an high series of protocols to the data bases of applications to conference settings for synchronization data links which showed how they tapped into her telephone services for long distance charges which she did not make. The broadcast series for her video would look something like ((sss5ssso x 6ssssss0) + (50 x 50)) to the CCAS. The items being in sellable condition were also the AMP of intensity to the look on the face of those attempting deceit.

The relationship to my Remembrance Day celebration services is in the progression of our Canadian identity. I believe the ecumenical traitor is from Holland. In the business of aviation, the Canadian constitution of land, sea or air elements proves the coalition of armies in a fourth dimensional component of the military campaign as Christians. Here there is no flag in the common-sense directive of interpretations. Do not use these words against me and do not judge me by your own thoughts or actions to the Mayor of any city state if the identifiable abstract of time is used for legal tender.

In literature the author is responsible for the characters developed. In real life, the parents are responsible for their children unless formally persuaded by law to show otherwise. For some, it is the marriage of security and the bible was the treatise to stop the illegal pilfering of our pensions. So how did the vasectomy finish become so invisible when the debates on abortion continue unreasonably and impassioned for all women in a court room. In my timeline, his first-born son's name was Philip and in the jealousies of the province of Quebec's male pattern baldness, the ecumenical debate will deprive the livelihood of another individual.

As for the Virgil person with no literacy skills or academic portfolio, I wondered why we were having to compete for the same pay if we are both employed with the same official capacity on behalf of the ER. Canadian economic studies represented to my efforts the honours title within the Province of my social publishing of local news articles. I was employed at the time of impact by the driver named Bruce. One cannot give more than what was offered so when I lost my employment due to this circumstance, the recovery could not be a garnishment of wages. That was the opportunity to speak for oneself and in the modern economy it gave me the chance to rise above the archaisms of earlier subscriptions of offenses to the wounding of feelings of umbrage. It is critical to one's health to become aware of these types of inequalities. If they are administrations to the social consultation to certain types of transgressions of the debate, then Moses would be the centerpiece for its recovery in civil society. In Canada the whup of Scottish culture showed our industrial capacity. Yet since King Richard was once a figurehead on the money account in commerce, the import and the taxes associated with those imports became a Rockwood for the Noel directories of NL electrical assemblies in the Toronto region.

I resent their implication of inclusion. The still born seal has nothing to do with my personal development since my grandfather's negotiation in the war was freedom in management. Canadians should not have to pay again for an air commercial incident on behalf of another country. Elaine is no longer a link to Exeter, Ontario and I am not the person with an iceberg floating in the ocean waiting to sink the Titanic. Erosion is not architecture so be prepared to propose the magnitude.

Banknotes are differentiated from the money account or coins. Manitoba is different from Saskatchewan and Ontario is different from Quebec. We are all various shades of flags under a constitution. Today it would be very difficult not to see the rivalry between a Mennonite, Sikh, Buddhist, Mormon, Hindu, Islamic jibba or Catholic office when living in an area devoid of an academic office. A supplicant is not just an adjective in a library of dictionaries. It is also the supplementary publication here to test the knowledge and form of our government. Since you were not there at the point of impact with that vehicle, it is not your tax account that you should be trying to divorce on behalf of the Mayor. The copyright is no challenge for the rightful ownership of a family lineage.

The term ground zero was used before the 911 attack occurred. It was used at the entry to a building in Smiths Falls. I still have the returned cheque for the publication of my resume CV. In this domain, my travel was not for leisure, it was for the wager of law.

I cannot believe how long the courts have made us suffer for the ties to an event that could never have been our fault.

CHAPTER FOUR

TEEN ATHEIST

My paintings are commissions. No matter what letter is sent to dismantle their supply, they will still be worth the effort. The atheist will search these entries to boycott their applications due to the English language syntax. Where bonspiel at one time did not belong in the dictionary due to the debates attached to its origin and spelling, I will someday belong in the value of the commerce in art.

Conspiratorially, I had no choice except to take the posting offered just like my own mother had no choice except to follow her spouse. The difference was that I made the manuscript a part of my journey. The court injunction to my employability would show that there are still a parliament of owls to say that every exit shall be equipped to provide illumination to an average level of 50lx at floor level. Furthermore, she was listed as an official delegate with the distinguished central office of information. That is where the writings are stored for legal status. As security director to the company, the presumption of the Chaplaincy to the family of sir names was a betrayal that could always be appealed by another in the default search directory of the banking community which attached the medical supply with those of the employer.

Thus, began the release of paintings to match the harms caused by the destruction of the medical records and the baseline of omission of her name to the absolute events of life. Island Custom Giftware, Jennifer Head, I Porteous, Peter S. LeBaron, Dallas Ali, Kevin J. Sealy, Al Gil and Fund Raisers. This is just a short list of nefarious people who contributed to the demise of the family unit in order to hold suasion power over the money supply. The CAA specialist listings to an address 105 route de la station, St-Antonin, QC G0L 2J0 was a memory which used a travel cheque to report the breakdown of the vehicle. It was the insurance which wrote the vehicle off and with that the driver became the victim of title skipping when her spouse was required to give all the names and addresses of her immediate family, including phone numbers and their relationship order from parental lines.

Nobody likes to be charged for crimes they did not commit and likewise nobody likes to be accused of something they didn't do when the accusation has been initiated as an Inquisitor into your professional space. Contrary to the food services industry, the fact remains valid that I would have created those works of art no matter if I were a resident in rural territorial divisions or not. As a resident in associations which appoints its office to a northwest enterprise of utilities providers, then it would be all too easy to attempt to throw her under the bus. As for her son, the Ravenview Project is not where I see his employment ability in this city of corrupt mayors.

For the democratic taxation of landscapes, I am not living in disorientation. I only have two children and I am absolute in realizing the fact that I have never had an abortion or miscarriage. We, as a family, have all been born in Canada where I have always paid my fair share of taxes toward the payroll account of people. We have built and been accredited for the functional building codes to interpret for our safety and security of our economic references to streets, roads, avenues, and drives from the Canadian perspective of ownership. You have no right to destroy what I own for a disreputable organizational service; especially those of a catholic rite.

I know what it takes to be an artist. However, I know nothing of what it takes to be an atheist. Maybe it is something that should be erased from the records of public health and safety like the word transgendered. It is not immaculate to be illiterate. It is illogical to be ignorant of your rights as a military individual and for that claim here, there will be a Hefey scribe to pay for your biases of freedoms. McPhee is the sir name to barter first. Sutherland is the second name with twin boys in the category of Tweedle Dee and Tweedle Dum. Finally, there are the Lairds who are knowing of the painting "Shades of Manes" comparing the visual expanse of the landscape into a synchronization of non-residency to the heritage tattoo. Two people are attached to death from the house number 101 South Drive. One was an elderly immigrant from Ireland and the other was a sibling who fell off the counter. From the aspect of moving forward across this country, I feel the ghost in that house has followed us as well.

The aircraft hangar felled was lettered D. The commanders in charge with reference to my copy of the Zimmerman telegram while protecting the innocent from the destiny of the unholy Jerusalem is using GMT 4,5,6,7,8. The legal brotherhood had no right to mar my placement here for the half hour time zone preference to NL. A&Vw Cook was ordained prior to the sources of meetings with Melvin Rose of the Ontario ministry of ordained persons to account for the archival document records of referencing military land. When referencing the leadership of who is more deserving of a placement in these areas of accommodation, I believe the Ordination had some preference over the boy whose name was William Barker. Now the only question at our dinner table of early childhood education was, "Just how cruel can all of you be to think that I would deny my only daughter the right to happiness just to exchange for a few spavin photos of naked political forms?"

Bills of lading consist of costs, freight and transport. Revenue Canada know the paperwork required to destroy all the goods that we have purchased in order to call a house a home. The Captain in charge of the NBCW team had an ally with the medical first aid instructors of the Brigade of St. John Ambulance drives on order of Jerusalem. Still today, on the side of negative GMT, I wonder how many vaccinations were administered to children from the hole in the ground as opposed to the children who were vaccinated and then billed by the office clerk to the province of their children's birthright.

As an afterthought to the personalities of people in the supply system of the Canadian Forces' Administration, there was the person Connie H who backed out on her obligation of hire by someone of the same rank as her spouse. She felt it was necessary to have the Captain of the food services industry to maintain her hierarchy of status in the pecking order of job security in opposition to the other rank Air Force members. I guess the organizational commitment of the valiant blue, uniforms were not good enough for her German born daughter of the army oath. I just didn't see the relevance of the velocity of the money supply making a difference as to which environmental uniform would be better suited to be an employer.

The distribution of money was related to government and she was aware of the consequences of working outside the esprit de corps. I don't think she realized just how big government was in the area though. Debt was highest among the teens and A5 was more than likely outside that jurisdiction of English civil society in the security of the corporate structure of the financial instruments. I also sensed the morose BMW would instantly create another variable calling on the healthy exercise program to stop the downward spiral of vacuous respects for the ghosts of the past world wars. Taxes in the past were what constituted the divine right of kings. So, the painting created was the true interpretation of what was seen at the time of the service attitude that came with the posting. With that painting on display even now in Toronto, there was no need to segregate the military family from the civilian populations. That being stated, there is an huge division among the legally married and the cult of common-law in the provision for blood money where the interpretations of taxation may or may not hold society hostage for their children on the streets.

I saw this coming out of these environs of socialistic spawns. The wolf is just outside your doorstep. It is too bad we had to fire them. Ethics ensures everyone knows the difference between criminal intent and accidental inventory. The syntactical rhyme scheme recited was ABCBDBD. The lullaby and the Christmas Carol authors were both of the same mindset around 1867.

Industry was what was required for the agriculturally poor soils of Victorian England. Canada proved to create much more opportunities for wealth based on merchant trades and traders. From those simple basic beginnings, I've also analyzed the bear trap in the exchange for those two children on the streets who were supposedly dead. After having to retrieve my files from the archives and seeing the damage done by the administration of the family unit, I also saw the destruction of the negotiable instrument for the accounting of spreadsheet operations. Sparks was the name of a pilot and it is the name of a walking street in Ottawa, the capital city center that also parties the same history to the D-Day invasion. Jan was the name of his spouse and the name offered to her in property management was Randy Romanan, a chief architect in charge of provincial codes to distinguish the year 1905 from the Breadlebane Road address as remedy to the situation already given in law to the marriage of the lamb. The street reflected the economic prerequisite of being based on the right to own property and secondly, the duty to legally fulfill contracts.

Yet, if men only needed a grade eight education in order to compete for a commission in the ministry where women instead were required to have completed at least a minimum of diploma to an high school education, then where is the basis of equality to the pay scale for military memberships across the spectrum of career choices under common-law wages except as a number in the criminal codes of Canada!

Mr. Vandroflare ran into the Chevrolet deliberately. This manor or local grievance wasn't the first attempt at the financial account of her personal deportment, and he wasn't the first European to have attempted this type of expensive exposure. This time the option of closure was just a shadow of the customers as clients since the asset was seconded with the passenger's personal information to the adjusters Bell and Young sir names as tabled experts in the case of claims against the crown or license plate crown against crown. Would the ministry of Generals at 279 Wellington Street just overlook her merit of eligibility to instead volunteer her status just so they could furthermore condemn and add to the hazing rituals of insult to injury. I believe that it is not ethical to legally remedy those illegally performed accidents based on a right to employment status of minimum wage-earning potentials. And this is still being done to our Canadian Forces personnel as the dental unit is a note in the margins of the Command structure.

Art is intentional and I believe that my Veritas Vincit is with absolute resemblances of the theory that there is justice for all including those whose names line the street posts of our maps. Johnson was the sir name of the deceased. In 2007, the political landscape brought together a throne speech for a minority government. Since then, the economic action plan has kept the conscience clear for most soldiers on the ground. Afghanistan is over though, and climate change is the new 9/11. The spiritual connection between the real and the physical is just a question of asking ourselves if we are better off today than before when our series of minorities were performance rated or rationally intended to vote for the federal power of Ottawa?

For some members of my family's history, partisan politics for pastors had been a good thing for everyone. Now though, the novenas of their spouse's devotion have been denied access to my accounts due to them having no civilized approach to government. If the Mormon case gets any more evident and if I should have to call for back up against criminal sex intents of that organization, then God help them.

Although I have a deeper understanding of Government now than when I wore the air force blue, I don't believe we have come out of commercialization with a more secure public record than yesterday's satisfaction of ratings by publications of newspapers and editorials. NAFTA did not do a very good job of keeping the political underpinnings out of the multinational corporate structures and depreciation did not have to threaten with radioactive annihilation. It is the same old President that caused the superpowers of the cold war to sign in on the best deal's benefactors of our student populations with the catholic school board trustees. The Berlin Wall, as a piece of landscape, came down in 1989. From the efforts of the people, I see that Canada should not allow corporate interests to be the benefactors of the entire population of students, their families and their businesses. The Tobin curse has a chair at the meeting place in history too as the license AD405 with the name of Blaize Ella Florence.

This is a genetic connection as opposed to logistics connection and it is where the link to the A5 was realized for code purposes. It is divisible. It is the beginning and the end as I can count to 5 on one hand. It is a respect for the person and not the noun or the invoice.

The President is not the Speaker of Canada. The people are speakers for Canada. We are a democracy graduated in both academia and technology. It is not beyond our level of articulation to certify our assets from our personal belongings as ownership. If Newfoundland wants to be presented as the storehouse of sex, scandal and violence, more than any other Liberal Party in Confederation, then the other provinces can judicially put an end to this exportation of claims to language as being anything but English. Claude was a Ross for the Bernier episode. I was the person who dedicated the results of those moles. The person herself was free to leave and we will choose our own habitat in the future instead of being made to rent by the Mayoral trainers of past pleasure-seeking instructors of a criminal mind. My instincts tell me that his Judah is the beginning of the end for the authority to the name Mary or Jason of the Golden fleece. Caila is a Newfoundland name to the daughter of a single mother. She is a threat to the legal namesake of our country's people with the man, woman and child to instead identify with an LGBT-Q community. That to me is a wrong Orchard arrangement where Canada is a proof that we are not a republic. We may have moved on in time, although we certainly have not moved to a better station in life. The BA of account knew that there was little room for error when it came down to identity theft. However, he alone made the choice to incorrectly enter her lineage on the baptismal certificate. Thus, when it comes to the truth about the tax and the burden of government, it will be on his conscience to have knowingly broken the covenant with God.

He could not be trusted again and the designation, if based on a slogan of decisions, suggested that the Reverend as a representative for all Reverends was a threat to all children in Canada. Nobody in the Canadian Forces would be immune from the evils he had inflicted on the woman with two children whose life was threatened needlessly for the Needham welfare. In the Rolodex of numbers after that was the MacIsaac name for immunizations before her children could attend school. Her spouse of husbandry literally knew that their time there would only be short lived. What German would not want to buy in on this hatefulness of Power to put her children in better favor with the releasing factor of past Philistines and Israelis in the area.

My published poem, since that ETA of commissions, shows the challenge to Viscounts. Although properly documented to the Province of Ontario, the beginning into the A5 code to the double entry account where in the logical progression of a system of profit for Canada was a measurement in the supply of manufacturing companies. The environmental economics of that measurement of the public utilities is likely due to the scarcity of the women to be able to clearly define what it was that was the threat when the Liberal agenda was cross referencing organ donations with the emergency measure's act.

Elaine is still a named party to the Arthurian Christmas steel. Ian Arthur of the NDP knew she was being framed for something that was not her fault let alone being stereotyped as a criminal. The ones responsible for misleading the public office of innocent people were the Justice Courts themselves based on the emails received that were knowing of the court procedures and not the Queen's Orders and Regulations. In this area of deceit were the names Flemming, Farihani and Batalla. It is about time these individuals were kicked out of school for causing the military family to be a constitutional death rate.

Sheri set us up purposely to bar the maiden names. For the media studies journals of the Queen's University, the bunting bag was not a primary economic sector. As for the Zinc of Crab enlightenment to the PE, I won't ever ask you to motion the privilege of an ambulance again in that province. My daughter won't either. So, to these two primary sectors of the economy, your name will be remembered as a predatory threat to the maintenance of a public bathroom stall with the message, "Go fly a kite."

CHAPTER FIVE

TIMES MEDIA PUBLISHING

We were required to have special licenses to operate the equipment under the conditions of extreme crisis. Having the police presence was not an issue. We were also all under strict protocol and after hearing the speeches on that postal code address, I realized that we could not go to our own homes. Furthermore, my daughter could not replace me as the "Sensitive Seniority" to a publication prior to her University degree status. Jocko was the unwed mother who would sometimes allow the dark side of our society to surface. There were even some who were using illegal drugs and I knew the insurance would not bail out these individuals. Thus, the files kept building until the international stories of abuse connected with the military to show all the flaws made by the administrations officers to entrap the most regal of our security markets. In this quinary level of home markets, you must learn to walk before you can run. The accident was an hard lesson to the performance of procurement where nobody was responsible for any equipment in the event of sabotage.

There were other females at this same location of quinary market evaluation and some with more experience.

Their remarkable illustrations of abuse are what we still call to account today. The artifact of my experimentation into photography showed the signs of the title I held. To the local political office, it was the fact of allowing other people to do the dirty work for you since the invoices could just be sent to a council that has a budget. Once the money is depleted, they will just stop payments to the local businesses and raise taxes the next year to make up the shortfall. The goal here was to prove your sense of self-worth and to get past the mountain of broken promises by the career managers especially those with a bias toward the tax account of Quebec birth rights.

Originally, she had been pushed off the deck by the pool. The cadet was not reported as she had just been a recruit with no experience in the grievance process. The gender association would not have looked good to all women entering that area of career development. Besides, she was an honours student and very proud of her academic accomplishments. She needed this career in order to survive and to not be given in marriage by the local clergy. So, in order to accomplish this task, she required the characteristics of a professional for the research and development of the macro environment. She also required recovery from the traces of a legal issue that could not be revealed to anyone with an insight into title skipping.

The training standards were not easy and her ability to swim was an accreditation to survival skills. As she refined the strokes of composure to the clothing that was a dead weight to swim a few laps, the technique became a comfortable measure to the other recruits who did not meet that standard of testing. I also seemed to remember the boot polishing competition as this was the first issue of government clothing. Although the conditioning of making a bed to certain specifications was a bit overwhelming to an intellectual community, the lessons were not intolerable. Considering that, we as a group, were not paying to stay in this public environment we also had no right to complain either. The administration of government forms allowed us to be paid, abet it was at a decreased level of minimum wage at a time when she had employment at a rate almost twice that level. It was not her fault to have been run over by a vehicle as a pedestrian. The only recourse available to her personally was to invest in one's own future.

The meals were prepared, yet they were not exactly accessible due to time appreciation. The men were allowed more privileges and access to meals were in excess to what they would have been given at home. Too much emphasis on the affordability of the cooking staff in order to make the capital investment worth a long term return possible. Her academic skills meant nothing here except that they were being tested against the male mind for the federal endorsement of Canada. It felt like an episode of pestilential eclipses which would mar her generation to the social communism of post war Russia. The sting of knowing this would not go away. It was a chronic issue that would persist throughout the whole life policy that they were assigned. Now the prejudice of either the motherland or the fatherland became the progression into the insurance industry. Evidenced as a first biblical character, she was absolutely enchanted that it was obvious to the writers of the group that Eve never really was the inventor of original sin. Her proof of this: The editor-in-chief knew the loyal partners craved a Presidential office. As any navy tradition dictated, what is yours is not yours and what is mine is always belonging to the father by me. This was a quaint little twist to the new testament bible study. Here with the memory of a one-time interview with her only grandfather revealed the schism of sibling rivalry to the nth degree. From this cozy Cape Cod postal address, the law he taught was drastically misinterpreted and now it was as equally misinterpreted by the hierarchy of military orders within each company.

A decision had to be made against the despots of the anna imports of both coastal regions. On the invasion of her protected, highly polished boot, someone in the staff etched the sign of the cross on the left toe of the boot. Knowing in her own heart that she was interpreting this discrimination as though an iconic catholic rite of progression into the compulsory service of psychological abuse. The boot representing Italy and its empire verses the British empire of capital resources in Ottawa's centralized governance. They were also offered free contraceptive prescriptions. Once she refused, the staff tested her integrity again by targeting her for minor flaws in the locker storage of her kit. Only once did she let it show how this affected her emotionally.

When the final dress parade was over and the convocation completed, without family or friends, she knew the fatherland actions would speak louder than words where nothing accomplished would have been appreciated even if the accident had never occurred. She knew the choice was for the betterment of life.

She vowed her children would not be orphaned characters to the misinterpretations of others. Her proof of existence was dedicated to the intents of Veritas Vincit and they would be found following the insurance industry professionals where they could be made found guilty of criminal justice for lack of intellectual property when fiction and non-fiction meet to discuss the particulars of ownership. True to these words in Latin text, Electra is the female version of Oedipus. It is very classic in literature.

In another interpretation of the Athlone GG of Canada, the Defence of the title Earl as opposed to Commander of Forces is an epic shift in the leadership principle for quoting the novel written by B. Howard: "The Chopper of Lucy Electra." Both references are requiring the vehicles to be written into the narrative with the evidence sunk in a body of water, like an embryo waiting to be borne by anyone with an investigative mind. This is how she became involved in the justice department. Since they were an experimental entry into the military campaign, she could witness first-hand the hatreds of the men; especially those within the rank and file. The attempt at undermining her driving ability by sending an unmarked vehicle to cross the road as her shift was completed to force her into the ditch made the function of critical truth to the facts a jumbled ledger of leechcraft medical accounts.

At the time of the purchase to the Chevrolet and the year 2001 to the driver's license of the personal insurance was the write-off of the company to the intents of title skipping local police units. The remark to say that, "My wife smashed the car.", was inappropriate and the premise of being haunted by yet another uninvestigated vehicle accident whereby the driver who was at the scene, was denied her constitutional rights by way of a proper investigation. It was a form of entrapment and the proof of the title skipping tort was not going to go away just like the cover page of this book. The socialistic state of the City to Brian or Bryan is responsible for the bulling of our financial tax account just the same as the author of the Lucy Electra character. In the fictional world, if the first name is unimportant then the second is like unto it. Formally, both the author and the character are rigidly identifiable to the purchasing transaction. Overriding the B rating in Howard's book about maintenance, since it certainly was not in the same league as the incorrectly vetted "Christian" name to an accident in Summerside, Prince Edward Island, her identity was a glyph.

The local public show of journalistic nuisance to support the political leadership which scrutinizes the security reports would show absolutely how the accidents were not her fault. Her liberty for the engineers knew the system well enough to say that the military police were a party to the complex coincidence of the message sent which spells I AMB Bics Major to support the Chinese Laundry Café of vapors for publishing the tax tables. Since their insistence on EU free press zones, nothing had opportunity for publication unless the NATO networks of Communications and Electronics museum experts forced the despatch of her son to the City of Toronto for a financial conference sponsored by the Dominion Bank of Canada.

The CELE officer was present at the time of arrival into Kingston. Stephanie is a half-sister to Peter and Zara Phillips to a Captain from a former wedding to the Royal Princess and the link to the historic Colleges and Universities in the area and we, as a family, could not have been any less informed about the structure of the political economy to the Beechgrove Complex and the Rockwood Asylum. She knew there were still two parallel lineages of this mythical Elaine and certainly Anne was not a fictitious offer to the Royal titles of Governor Generals. In our lifetime, one Elaine is dead at the invitation to those Elaine's in the riding of Egmont. More recently communicated, the genuine preference was to the two Kings of old for both their extremisms and atheists alike. It seems the Jin and the yang of legal and racial torts to control the gender qualifier for the President is for sure biased to the nth degree.

She spoke to him in his lonely exile, "There is a heaven. It's just not with you."

The Christian Wendy that was the focus of a child's death had nothing to do with our service records. Yet, she was a performer to the womb of the confession as part of the catechism. Here her Electra siblings were a recidivism guarantee of automatic channels to advertise sponsorships. This was the motivation for my measurement of support for my children to be given a clean break from the Saunders' predestinations of oppressions due to investigations which do not base their findings on facts and the evil intellectual war which unfolds to the pilot of a Sea King with a desk job in Ottawa did not have the TOSH Veritas Vincit of the Canadian legend, Billy Barker at their side.

Killam was sent to Germany for his betrayal of her name to the supply of fuel to military aircraft. Apartheid had nothing to do with the legacy of the physical persons verses the Ball of fictional characters inside the financial posting of message center activity. As Canadians, in a literary listing of world bank registries of husband investors, it is not a good idea to break up a family unit by selling them out of their homeland. Besides, we should never have had to quarrel in the English language with such an enemy as the Colonel B's of military ID cards. As the author of certain architectural drawings, there is only one poem to express my discontent with the government for not stopping the abuse before it became an epidemic.

Moonlight is
Thumbnails in the
Month of October
Emails of crescent
Smiles at the gym
Perfected atomic numbers
Half stream beacons
In marble covers
Describing rotary phones
To students measuring
Redwing scholars
Sent to credit wins
Portraits of traffic geniuses
In structures of metal bliss
Whiff of fortunate aroma
Orbs of oscillating light
Blue as cultural bondage
Tyranny to accost Social justice cowards
Pretty brides gone missing.

Amalgamation is over for this city. No offences until now. No defence either to the property ownership of our titles. This poem has not been given anything more than just a statement at the end of the gender slur. It was written after the proclamation by a Mayor which reduces the bride to nothing more than a complicated debate for the Courts. I resented the person to speak on behalf of all residents and taxpayers. My status to make the best of a bad thing deserved some credit as a finishing touch to our democracy. Contrary to our past Remembrance services which marked the 19th anniversary of Europe's battle on Vimy Ridge was the loss of our belief in the matrimony of our parents and then their partners before them.

The Mayor had gone too far with the ecumenical debate for which we found ourselves confronted with in the modern world of investment planning. Canada was not at war. Afghanistan was at war. Working in a democracy gives many people all kinds of choices and it is usually a courtesy, as military agents of property, to confront the crisis the same way we encounter the economy of an automobile accident. We should always work as best we can to prevent further injury especially if you are the force holding the weapons of assault.

Maybe it is the truth of Einstein's existence which rallies the cause. There are no O words in the Jewish alphabet. She wrote his country's name out in the balance. Her teacher had been in that area much longer than they ever would. She wrote to protect their landscape. She wrote to improve the likelihood of a future comfort to an enemy oppression. It is one of those things that say, she pardoned and protected a little for the time spent there. The logo, however, is not hers to claim and so the bruises are a point in which she found a way to address the frustration of losing a parent in the same way I felt about losing a spouse.

That account of the purple exists to show there is also a reason for changing the middle name on the grounds of identity theft. All things being equal, it is a choice I had to make alone, without biases. It is an international approach to a constabulary in the same day as the brokers and still encourages the history of departure at the airport.

Now that I remember the refusal of the drugs issued as sensitive unwanted solicitations, the seasonings of cumin, basil, rosemary and summer savory were the replacement values in the cupboards of our home to protect the aroma of all seasons to the only property he had left to salvage: the province itself. L.M. Montgomery wrote about its beautifully pictured spirituality to that element of time and place. We approached this future event after having visited this place just one more time before her mother died in 2005. This is where we first saw the apparition of a ghostly spontaneous thing above the cross on the ground as we walked the length of the beach.

I could never be associated with the element of fire and the nays of Sioux showed their features of ido along the documented lands of Meacham's atlas. The land was so well documented in the position of contract law that the ghostly relationship to our world avowed its irreconcilable contractions of existence. From law as well, this message did not mean to go ahead and insult my intelligence for the offering of a peace in direct evaluation of the male coming out of the 275 Wellington Street address with a marijuana cigar in his hand, smiling as a token to the Ministry of Health officers in the same building.

I am a legal registration. Some of these citizens are not. When Jodi was born 26 November, that painting would be the proof to my lineage and my property to the province and not hers. I still am apprehensive about the birth of Prince

William of England. He has timed out now, so the issue is not an assumed one time offer to the Order of St. John of Jerusalem at Memorial University. The painting will not be offered again.

Mathew is a noun. It may also be spelled Matthew as much as William may be Liam. Personally, I would have stayed away from the name Mathew. My research in respect of the languages were in order to respect the system as was designed to be understood by the ownership of land titles. My conclusion is that there could be no end to the Governor General & Company. The style should develop the artist and the artist should develop the property and it is then that you will understand your subject when you see it appear before you. I made it colourful. I took the management position and got rid of the neurosis for it is a plague from which one will never recover. I do not regret standing up for the decisions I have made to protect myself if I must correct legally a wrongful conviction. My son is innocent and cannot be blamed for acts of indecency which took place before he was born.

The cross in the red sand of my childhood memories was a saving image for us in this final year of representatives of his house and the occult. Liard is also spelled with a Lane to the registration where Dr. Richardson was the special guest at this ceremony of real death. She brought with her the little manuscript of the school board trustees to utilize the capacity of life, a consistent expert authority to her existence where there may have been none before. He was born in 1934. His witness stood for a flag; but it was not the leaf of Canada.

The naming of the Corporation began after this ceremony.

Almost with absolute certainty, when somebody new enters in life, someone else will leave. The taxation of this country and its many peoples shows how the couples without children may be a part of your memory as a parent that is in pursuit of government without shame. This cerebral challenge was not something I wanted to wear. It was something more of the vividness of reality from the many forms of ideological standpoints of becoming a nation requiring the supremacy of government.

This hall of government was seen by many who have had to trek here into the heart of their government's expectations and those who collectively have found that their profound statements were derived from a deep recession of time where the stable expanse of the cathedral and its light upwards towards the sky gave the viewer the impression that this was the place to be if you wanted to understand the universe. It did not however want you to see the part of a community in discontinuity in the dignity in human life by taking one life in exchange for another.

We came to the understanding of speaking. We came here because the people in the intelligence community wanted to use our texts for their indifference to the changing demographics and dynamics of the partners of elected offices. The Miter was in decline now. These insights of importance of government positions to our experiences in leadership would be a threat to a family to reassurances in their future discourse. The threat of being voided ever so deliberately with the history as an estate of the grave markers in training with weapons to an escheat of Cardinals awaiting their academic fate made me a civil acclaim to an unstable uniform. In the chamber of our skilled division, we had no other choice except to redesign our decided placement with the perspectives of motifs without dealing with the demons of vacancy in the rivalry of a King of Arms.

In Canada, the ground is broad, extending from the heights of lands we own. The imprint of schisms on our souls from war is an everpresent creative tension among the justice's numerical path of postal codes. Also, the absence of our history among the philosophers of the Senate meant that the apprehension of motif in the gules of arms was a conversation of a union like the government itself associated with a constitution. This treaty is an impartial coherent to the image of John. He, being a design voidable to the beginning of a purpose of redesigning from the exposure of outer space instead of the Athenian fables of our sisterhood to the name of Jesus. Neither is capable of survival in the long-term analysis. Unlike the fallen soldier who never dies, immortality is his according to Sam Hughes. He is an elegant element of the human imagination. He is only changed by a username. He cannot dictate the antique markets or the asylums of abandoned children. He is far too distant in our minds from the Rothias surnames of the Domesday Book of 1066 and he does not equate himself with the tribes or individual members of the common stem of civilization. Yet he is a part of the democracy and of the bureaucracy of formal identification and accountability. The practicality of his life and my stories go together at the bar of arbitration for a proof that the writer is a different form of messenger than that of the orator.

When the solitude of the vocational cobblestone of the city is viewed against the pagoda elevation of garden surveys, this would be the time to begin your shelf. You can live without John. However, you cannot hold up against a truth that begins with the study of life or the trees of treason to the landscape of reality. If I could imagine, maybe at the time of our gravesite oration that John is clinging to the face of a rock cliff, what are the choices in thoughts? Does he choose the point in life of his weightlessness in the womb which gives him the sense of reality of having lived among the unicorns, even though he knows that it is a fictional being or does he choose the image of the protectionist works that has lead him to the image of a self-preserving sandstone sphinx?

The details of events shown here tells us of an event with which statistics have invaded the ethics of our personal belongings and our choices as government minds would rebuke the passion of Christ as did so many socialist writers of our common past. Are we going to be left with our worldly goods to make our homes deep in the woods or live in the openings left in our ancient cathedrals clinging to the upmost spire to be enlightened by the possession of knowledge stylized by the expectations of powerful police forces?

This document is the treaty I offer to the muse of the Kings. This is a story about the heart of an artist whereby she is not the dauphin child of a precious sun god in the procession of Popes and she certainly is not the vanity of power lines in the brotherhood of dental records for the DNA exchange of currency among the bouquets of poems she writes for the death of her lover on the compass rose of surnames.

When it comes to the civil war of first names, David is a man's name. In our modern world, how many bridges to we need in order to control traffic? How many tanks do we need in order to exercise the celebrity of a marriage between the fleur-de-lys and the sovereign? I can only answer these questions by stating that John has come into our world to do what was intended to be done and his shadows are a single blessing to the landscape protecting our souls as we are in absolute fact. Much of his being known to me is by accident, not experiment. Like the statues in my grandfather's memorial book and the Vimy grounds available to us today, he would be upholding the dignity of human life past the waters of Isis.

The Captain of fifty is an honourable man. Form is an artifact of certainty. It is engraved like a sealed oath. Yet the name John is a name of vision, even like a nightmare brought forth into the future of known properties such as the owl, raven, and dove. As artists, we become immortal in the oils of our landscapes and the unicorn is the vision of our spirit in lavender fields which desires to be a part of every living thing. The forest is her child; a parable from which we begin to write and survive. The Master leads us out of the forest to become acquainted with the person we have become. The story behind the story is Beland and I know the victory over death.

CHAPTER SIX

BABIES FOR HIRE

The character of Jesus in the Christian theology was meant to solve the problem of hiring children to pay for their offspring in the taxation of portraits and royalty maps. The law is a progression too. There are shifts in resources and the pavilion of tax tables in Canada, two Canada, do not apply equally to all. The political rift became a slander for many women and the entry into the old testament Judah and Micah was a personal threat to the royalties of England and Europe proper.

I say this with the address of the exiled in the penitentiary of Asylums to the Rockwood property where their conditions of bargaining with the ownership principle was bankruptcy, insanity and death. That is what Wendy had drawn me into with the Foster Parent Plan. My reference to protection of our resources was that all three fates could not happen at once. It is an impossible truth. The attachment of the fraud was documented and an appointment to the bench was for having two children. Solace to the sibling connection and the Princess Royal, are the names Pamela and Angie in the administration of the social insurance investigation files; not fils of the Brotherhood collective bargaining agreement. The consulting practitioners of the Attorney Generals Offices, as I see it, rests with the Canadian soldiers who have participated in a peace for the Middle East. When the extremist's state, "No man cometh unto the father but by me.", I can clearly counter the entrapment as being gender biased.

This community was testing her knowledge of constitution, not locomotion.

Newfoundland and Labrador do not have the same pilgrimage status that Israel does, and a tour of duty for six months does not mean willful abandonment by the spouse. A person would have to be blind to not realize that fishing off the coast of Labrador as a child should not coincide with the military attaché for a tour of duty in the Middle East. As Prince Edward Island, once St. John's Island, will never again be annexed with Nova Scotia, I believe Confederation should stop the berating of our women in military uniforms. Where were you at when I was at the corner of Botsford and Mountain Road.

The political slander is returned. Dene was once published in the Kingston telephone directory and it now has been replaced by the name of Holland's Oene. I hardly think that when it comes down to a translation, that the deliberate attempt at an exorcism to the Catholic faith by garnishing the wages of our deserving military was a form of religious sabotage. The preventable omission of his actions to instead accuse an innocent victim of circumstance, when it comes to the operation of motor vehicles, to further disgrace her character with those of a Jen's Monk.

This is not an academic test. There isn't even any resentment. There is just the truth to my ownership in property. I am not as dumb as you think I look Mr.

Bradshaw. The slander is noted and as a police constable, you do not have those qualifications which allows you to put that comment down as part of your own words. There is no literal connotation of spoilage to write off vehicles when it comes to government title skipping. You also had access to every military record in every province in Canada to the archives in order to accomplish this dirty deed as with the Janus of unwed mothers included in the category of women as minorities and aboriginals to hire. Inclusive of the Ontario Attorney General's Office is the Health Services Industry to entrap the military professional and to further the bereaved of many a poor soul from the financial tyranny of hate crimes. The name Constable Bradshaw will forever be the demon of title skipping torts in this country we all call Canada.

This was a nasty thing to do to my family and my maiden name to a Section 91 and 92 of the surname Rose. I was asked twice about a baptismal name in trust with the security of our country to my ownership in property. Yet, the certificate of baptism was purposely incorrect for a political suasion between the Reverend and the Church for which he was given a position of authority.

My mother, at her death, was butchered for another's life to be divorced.

This was an unforgiveable slander to all Canadians and all women who have believed in our democracy. The economic substitute of a great person with that of a slattern calling for death by constitution is a threat we should never have had an opportunity to write about. Our children are not the consumption behind the dragon of St. George when your Mayor decides to manipulate the fraudulent names of innocent children to their mother's maiden name. Therefore, Teresa had to be the anna of India.

Liberalism doesn't mission a position when trying to make the populations act any more octogenarian than the transportation of evil men. The artist is comforted by the new works created by a peaceful errand into the future condition for the contents of the completed works of truth to the accident investigation which will prove beyond infinity that it was not her fault. She would never have named her son Benjamin. That is an educated statement from the academic portfolio of her account of property.

A-PM-245-001/FP-Z02 is the same in both official languages. Nota means to reinstate our knowledge of the Indian citizens to reject all the candidates in an election. This is what the Company TRJ stands for in our peaceful community and our Mayor is responsible for its anarchy. All things are not equal in the debate of war with the qualifications that are universally true to the notion of Canadian Law and Business Administration. I am Canadian and so is my son. The personal vehicle is off limits to payment of debt owed by the city to its citizens when it comes to premature death.

Since the Great Seal is both a version of the French/English publication, I wonder why it was that I should be the only one to have to address the torts which are options that have implications of Mafia suasion powers to the test of time.

The Single One Revisited

Secrets scattered like ones who wait
Suffered more than ye
Come to steal your bids at hand
Break vows, so there's more for them to see In shattered
migraines big on slatterns.
Rescue!
Give me ale for your life instead
Close that door. Open the devil's gate
Archdeacon of pantheons
Relinquishing single reports.
Remember who served first
It certainly wasn't Gordium
That spark master in charges for souls
Take Adam's misery beyond Autumn's plate
Spare me even further beyond its Holt Success is but a mark,
a torus Bane of Justice or Honour of Eden.
Proportion.

Our government is unaware of these words. It is a
situation that provokes the history of our literature with
my Fiche de Competence du Conducteur to any military
vehicle after the entry date of 22/2/93 for which we will
swear and will witness, as absolutes, a reserve protocol to
regulate the wages of my industry standards. As for the
Tulchinsky of Queen's history and the tenure of the bench,
this is an extreme statement to the conditions of abuse,
harassment and fraud. The priority is to limit this premise
and to accommodate the two's bills from the provolone
gifts of Christmas lights and family celebrations. The

identification of the military 404 by the Administration attempting to bastardize her children at this location of operations privileges, was a sage that turned into a shaman.

All my poems were written unto me. It was the paintings that were given for the public view. The lullaby was justification to the spelling of my maiden name, correctly in all its forms. D. Ross was an epaulet for the first-born Christian with the name as Benjamin as proof of his death without a cause. As for the Sutherland clan, psoas joints don't always need replacements. Just make sure you don't schedule me in. Your people were in a dire condition and we healed your distress and you tried to beat my children in the system of naval reserves with the army of vehicle CFRs and ECCs in order to accomplish the dirty deed. I gave you an oil painting. It is not a restricted covenant to convince the people of your family that my children are innocent beyond any doubt in any address of postal codes across this country. They are protected. If in doubt of this manuscript, go back to the beginning. Pick up what was forgotten. If you must travel, beware of the names Berczy and Woolsey with an obelisk.

The artist was warned about the danger involved with portraiture. She had a childhood ambition though and the bumpy flight into the military family was a conclusion to the inert power of a Gulag D-Day revival. Just because she never lived outside the country of her origin, she did not have to be so deprived of services as to render the persuasiveness in formality of UN replacements as unskilled incompetent labor.

This story is rooted in the kindness to the strategy of a prose of whisperings to the Kings at the cross of Canada's

Sacrifice. She gave the bouquet of that same honour. Her mother's divorce, in her last rights, was the trail of fraudulent men to the Road of her daughter's enemy. This story may not last forever in the archives of copyright, but it is a beautiful gesture of delegates from the remembrance of this D-Day number 6. Unlike some other forms of resolutions that will wilt and die, this one will take on the distinction of colour from every description that has always been used by artists throughout the ages. As graduates to the border of consequences for those who were wrongfully convicted, the effort of assembly may not always be at the graveside ceremony.

She accomplished the spiritual reality as a known military delegate. The transfer of oil colour to a reproduction of the same idea is the word beautiful. In remembrance, a symbolic wooden cross was captured in a snapshot on the shoreline as either a premonition or artefact where she and her daughter walked in communion one day. The highest authority was with them always. Canada for us was calculated in 100 years of publishing crediting the opportunity to registration before there was ever such a thing as a Great War. My grandmother is now at peace in the heaven known as Prince Edward Island.

CHAPTER SEVEN

VISCOUNTS TWO TO UNION STATION

Once you have been tried by the justice system there is no denying that you will always be in contempt of court. Maybe that is why we prefer cats instead of rats, or dogs, or pigs. Industry leaders did not exactly understand transportation in the regard of losing an airport. Since we were always given an invitation from the message center, we made the portion of our togetherness as part of more than one province. Yet, when there are two children only in a multitude of incriminating emergency communications involved, then why blame me for the scattering of useful resources. So, if you think this written account is going to let the incrimination of the reality of ownership, you will be very sad with the ending. Although this is just a story, there are contracts which will abolish the Woodside last name. Liftow is limited to the first digit, not the whole hand. That is why it is probably more appropriate to ask someone to wiggle their toes. As part of a security clearance, it respects the fact that you are there to see the physician for something more trivial than complying with the request.

Accidents happen. However, before you go around in accusation of everybody and everything, just train yourself to understand that we have a complicated system of inventory whereby solutions in the sequence of events must prove that initially it was not your fault even if on your own property. If you must challenge another higher authority in context, make sure they have the same opportunity to report correctly. The children with an obelisk mentioned did not have the gift of speech as a basic text. The Reverend was unworthy of his position and the pay associated with its accommodation. The dictatorial persuasion of making people act outside of their primary or secondary markets is unfair and an unwanted solicitation. I can see the reason, as a species, to want to bring recruits into that game of numbers and I even understand why those men would want to expose themselves in front of young girls. However, it is unacceptable since it is an unwanted solicitation. I will not invest in the health care system since one can obviously see how the trademark has failed the nursing profession.

He is where the first is not the last and the last is not the first. In Jewish symbolism, the TM is not in Toronto anymore. There is a reference to the Mafia though so the delivery of my speech from the Abscission is a lineament of the attendants to the details of my literature in the Canadian themes of maple leaves. It will show how safe you can be in the blink of an eye.

The politician is an example of a pseudo-event and a fire is an example of a real event. Death is a real event. So that leaves the aphasia a detail to be determined by demographics. The Reverend M. Rose was aware of what he was asking for and the person, myself, in innocence of the circumstance of death, was as sympathetic to the occasion as could be. In comparison with the military Reverend, he too knew of the certificate of betrayal using the wrong surname. I hope he likes the Beechgrove Complex. It is a place in the Ontario government which practices the Electra and Oedipus psychology. Anyone who had just two children in the gender of one to one is libel to a written statement of the crown to bastardize the female mother of the family unit proclaiming the LGBT community as a force to be accepted by everyone.

If using a psychological profile to injure a person's reputation written by a department that has nothing to do with the investment in a residential single-family dwelling, then the constitution of our country is a failure to all Canadians with ownership of their personal belongings.

The crown is a common breeding ground for such concepts as ethical, logical, legal and agnostic. At the time of questioning, there wasn't another person in the building. Thus, the Reverend is guilty since he was the person with the authority of public trust to the lesser ranks of the organization and seniority. The incorrect lineage for the person named was a breach of the office of all Chaplains and equally dishonest was the threat made by Constable Bradshaw.

The proof is more meaningful in the finance where the kiosk is also a pavilion as like the cross of sacrifice on Parliament Hill where each idea and charitable donation was specific to the health of the public's interest to make sure people were treated without bias even if not supporting the LGBT community. In visual definition for the Defence and Federalism by negation, please see the CPP losses and the immigration status of people from Cardiff Wales. The comparison status to Harry Wales would be a quinary market of global research grants. That is another reason for my absolute statement of not being a catholic. I have also considered the facts of delving into the dissembling confessions of security guards.

I am knowing an higher convocation than just the evaluation of the intents of selling someone out of their property. Immigration began in Canada around 1812. In the history of a correction before the curse, the public school could not contradict its existence either. Therefore, to evaluate a to b in the acceptance of a Mayor, one must determine the preference of something other than a Mayor with an ability of opportunity to speak on your own behalf.

The Mayor is not any more mathematically correct than I am. I do however have more qualifications than they do for the wage rate of my resume submitted. To ignore this fact is just as dishonest as was the police constable's remarks for the female having to protect her personal property.

An IUD is not the same thing as an IED. Yet when it comes to methods of entrapment to staff administrations, then the taxpayer has the right to report the illegal nature of the intents to ruin the reputation of the mother and to abuse the rights of our children to government insurance in order to gain access to the privilege of divorce, by consignment to the French language of catholic priests.

Tom died on the rock just as his father had before him and now, he too has returned to settle a sibling affair. We are not a catholic family and I am equally not atheist either. The name of the book called into question the authority of the term "National Identity" and not the book bound by the publishing community of NIV's distributions in local bookstores. The name Abegweit was different than the origins of Jenny and Kali. I had to be absolute within the legal office of my oath of office. I had to learn to think about the patterns of random old Vics. Claire was sent to Germany and she never made it back to Canada alive. Europeans do not like natives. Now my father will not be returned to Canada. For that ghost of my mother's reputation as a nurse, Elaine will see to that.

All these things have taken place and will not be forgiven. Lily and its castings are not supporting the dawn of commissars. We've promised never to allow the people of our country to be commanded by another army and to relive a City of Fredericton as though it were a Saint John of biblical Heredic revelations is not going to happen as long as there are CBC archives in order to escape the telephone directory to each key political party from our CRA accounts.

News reels and replays are not bargaining powers to the building materials used to house those occupants of 705 Division Street. You do not even have a market for which we use to employ our citizens, yet the reporters seem to think they have a priority when it comes to decisions that affect the whole community. Pluralistic persuasion based on an illegal cult is wrong for the individual. That is why polygamy must remain illegal. I believe the name Manessah would be allowed at a time when one realizes that there is only one death and there must be a power to stop that false witness before somebody decides to make it a fellow at the bar. I can't in any logical diversity of universities claim to want to convert to an illiterate form of illegal persuasion.

Just as a vasectomy is a form of illiteracy, the subscription to the contraceptive opposite of the brand name Viagra tells us we have a double standard of solutions for humans. The question that rests on the shoulders of the justice system is, "Did he have to kill her?" as opposed to what happens after the point of a public death.

I am third in line to the Manessah Prayer. It is a tertiary guarantee in contrast to the baron with his stepchildren for the vision of Jacob's ladder. He was a guardian to his time. Although we have risen above empiricism and sophism, the Bernice schism shows how the structure of votes in analytics is far different than the structure of truth: The Vicegerent though only calculates wins to the ownership of life in this modern painting as it creates its own time and its own place.

It was not an experiment of work forces nor was it a secular right for political points of interest. The paintings should not be expropriated from the author as they are an inventory item. There is no need for the government to ruin the reputation or blacklisting their depreciation as though it were a capital postal code. The city itself is a registered threat to the authority of the author as the management is the creation of litigation into the concept of war museums. To that end, the artist is employable and the security report where the UN understands the lodges of recreational hunters, the analytics also shows how the bullet proof vests are just a fancy garment for men to boast about in the locker room. The artist will always be returning to Canada since she knows that the code name of Ground Zero aka 911 was mentioned in boardrooms before the attacks took place. It just took a little time to make the theory a reality concept in 2001. In imaginary constructions, old Nick informally means the devil!

Oleographs are technology images and they were used to supply the markets with a cheap colourful print of oil paintings. They decrease the value of the original painting so the investment in the oils themselves are relegated to a niche market where the public decides whether to invest in the name. Osage Orange is an hard thorny tree bearing wrinkled orange-like fruit which has a durable orange-coloured timber. I gave my son's Doctor this painting for the benefit of showing that his mother does have talent. His own studio had a print which used an apple blossom awarded to him by the Asian community of Queen's University. In comparison to my studio, we were void of any public accreditation. That is the difference between the two levels of academic portfolios.

OMM means military merit. Outflank means to get the better of another. Personally, I believe that marketing gives far too many undeserving Canadians the best years of our children's lives. The Doctor was not going to let his appointed child be befriended by the casual few years of obtaining a placement to my son's entry into secondary school training. Turning the Taurus of time appointed for his extracurricular training, I had seen the bar as a last condition for consideration. Instead he was given the Old Bill as a slang reference to police where NICS is a military acronym for NATO Integrated Communications Systems. There could not be any level of willful blindness to the community which assumed a naming right to these assumptions of career expectations.

I could not be attached to this type of communist and socialistic mindset to imprison my children with the politically attached status of titled Liberal Speakers of the house to this President's Choice TM. The oil paintings were my knowing of the sense of entrapments to both the mother and her children. Therefore, I shredded the checks, knowing that the third party pshaw could close the bar at any time. Yet, you could not stop the commerce of the artist. A divided comment for the ensign would be to say to the community, "Do not oppress my security with the constitution of America first." The cult of scrounging the soroptimist in management with the SI units of volunteer women.

Jenny is a name within the region of Senators who participated in the Manchausen Syndrome by proxy. Burghley is the sur name of the Queen Mother's administrator where we all have been summoned to our pay. Israel is now an independent state where if twins were born in the one of each gender category and as a condition of Judaism, since marriage is not a sacrament to which requires a formal divorce, then in the spirit of competing Olympic events, the male will kill the female.

Captain Mark Philips was lucky to have kept his rank after his divorce from the Princess Royal considering the Burka as an international garment of oppression. It shows nothing of the people's religion. So, to continue with the proofs of the English system of Administrative Law in Canada, is the deceased's decision to knowingly allow the partnership to sign as a matter of free will. Thus the signature on the piece of art in this sense is more mobile than the person called the author and the arc of the Covenant to Abraham who a lineage that went terribly wrong in the end if you were to explore an insurance claim to the wonders of wealth management into today's shifts in treaty organizations. In this reasoning, two heads are not better than one as the economics of scarce resources becomes a burden to the individual after their death. Thankfully none of the portraits hanging in the Parliament Buildings of Canada depicts their electors sitting on an ass.

We have been modernized and would not even think of this type of long-standing image for an administration. Yet we do have a problem with the dumping of those old ideals. So, if I saw both my children to be of a catholic league of avatar characters and they were in the military element of the sea, then the perfect murder will be initiated for she will not have a record of her own existence. The threat came from the firefighting training she took on the premises of Chester Street showing how the Reverend has set forth to the accused parents as elements in the spirit of the aviation industry, his own anthology recording the presumed risk of his old PMQ. It also proved how giving people toward a cause that is seeded in debt financing has no exit unless you find a way to build a secure way out. For that reason, the business card has shown the maple leaf as the abscission. I am a certified Canadian for as long as I am alive with the proper signing authority within the provinces of myself and my children thus preventing the anna of India from entering into a contract with the Karenina of Tolstoy.

In fact, many times I have gone back to that same bookshelf trying to discern whether it was I to have accidentally misplaced the book by leaving it on the floor. Yet the book is somewhat hidden among the other classics on that same shelf. As an act of remembrance, it would have taken a great amount of effort to place that book somewhere in total innocent strategy to attend other matters and to forget that the book had been reviewed by the artist: right after the evening of watching a program about an artist who dies in jail who was innocent of committing any crime. His daughter becomes the haunted person to set the record straight and it leads to her ownership of the very valuable art collection. To say that I was intent on rereading the novel would not have suited my personality as I have never reread any book on my shelves unless it was a reference "teacher/ student" book.

As for the mystery admitting that there is a possibility of ghosts, this concept has never entered my head at any time in my academic training. Even in the military situations of manuals and training in old archaic bunkers, there was never any hint of apparitions to document a foreshadowing conclusion. So that knowledge is an affirmation to the quality of the training obtained while in a military uniform.

An investigation in the household also shows no one recalling having touched the books to leave one on the floor. Although I did note that it was in the winter of 2005. It was cross referenced later in my memory as the license plate number of my father's vehicle, AD 405, in Prince Edward Island. It was also approximately one month before my mother passed away.

While in my own discreet accrued knowledge of her existence, her maiden name is a security question often reminding me of the banking community. For the memberships of her military connection, I saw this mystery book on my floor as an opportunity to add to the multitude of urban legends and I salute the day in which I was made a victim of a vehicle pedestrian accident in that same city of her mourning. So, the flow of clavicle broken bone of my son, is the unforgiveable standard of harassment of police constables today.

In my house, I am the forest child.

The forest is a soft
Mellow light
That abodes
In the corner
Of my house.

Its erotic sound
Fades away
To a dot In the sky.

CHAPTER EIGHT

BOOKS OF CLEAN STATEMENTS

I told the hospital staff that I would write the story. This is that story of abuse so disgustingly vulgar that even in our new addresses of postal codes, a ghost will haunt your floors. This is not superstition like those of the thirteen floors. It is about the deception of a lineage that had already been passed on from the War of the Roses. I was only a little girl when my father berated me on Christmas eve. As my parents were exchanging their gifts, their conversation began with my mother analyzing the gifts and the honesty of us children to believe. In truth, the eldest of us children had known what was wrapped to be given to me and suggested that one gift may have contained more than one item. So logically, since my brother was the chocolate thief in my grandmother's chocolates, that I must have cheated and opened a present before the sacred day of Christmas. I judged that it was still not worth the berating of a child to such a horrible perception of their intents with the ability to answer to the high courts, the truth behind the accusations. Many other situations occurred while growing up with their family which showed how this rebuking escalated to the point of no return. Thankfully, the Jewish community did not celebrate Christmas.

To this day, I resent the city of St. John's Newfoundland and Labrador. I will never return anything to this confederation. The fact that this little girl was ostracized by the patriarch of the ownership in land was a rival concept that would not go away. Furthermore, the hatred continued with her parent's siblings, even unto the courts of probate to exclude her in the best wishes of an afterlife for the wedded couple which has spilled over into the bastardization of my own two beautifully attended children.

The description of the King and Queen of England and France on the memorial of D-Day celebrations between two rival countries in Canada is a remarkable show of how peace can be maintained in the future. Yet the stories of authors warn of the innocent and of the spiritual gender of old testament interpretations. I do not interpret. I am the zenith to the command of authority to the words written as an element of the law Actus Reus. Studio 14 was a commercial image sent to her by her mother and it was used as a form of blackmail to the long line of accountants in the banking industry of her maternal mother. If this was a power for her life, the chronicle of truth would be absent. The link to Exeter was the weakest of the military posts. Elaine: "You won't be coming after me." I am a very distrusting passenger to the majority recipients of the poet command. As the role of Administration to prove the Arts and Letters of despatch to her son, she felt it was like winning the lottery within a walled city of unwedded Ansels: Wendy insisting still that they had inserted a chip in her nose.

The medical aspect of immigration was a debate which saw the indoctrination of Canadian women into the American work force. The posting was all too actuated for my competition. Her mother now is dead. The mark of the obelisk could be written or omitted, yet it would be recognized by the educated classes. There was no claim either to the motherland of history to her era. My business was now worth well over the amount calculated as the discussion of the gentiles with a Baccalaureate of Roman numerals to the Chapters of the NIV.

He used his alma mater against her only spouse in a most vulgar showing of flesh and blood. I guess the Jewish menorah was a form of exorcism to continue with the motto within the Liberal caucus. She now insisted that Art was not a form of entertainment and the title of a sports coordinator could not be reactivated considering the facts. His license number not an accommodation in any other province of engineers except for the one where she was buried. As the act of completing the final note on the lullaby, the tern AD was stricken from the courts of records. The program was now at its final gravity. Ground zero was inappropriate yet it was a catch phrase used by the officers at the time. Here rules of measurement are like currency: make sure you invest wisely. Canadian currency is clearly distinct. Her design did not pass the competition though.

Chapter X.

Every book should have a chapter that reaches this conclusion. Anything less would not be worth the effort. Just be sure to consult with the publisher before using the words of language programing journals. In this book the name Sasha was the trade for the army Captain. She was born in Germany and we had no such experience. In the list of all or any first born persons, Laura had been quite determined to reach the Sargent acronym to a logistics network of SGT. Octavian, on another level of languages, left his mark with the arresting of all their careers by allowing the Command to post without giving credit to the CD merit. Her strategy on the French language, right or left, was to be informed of every provincial statute connected with the offering of a promotion to the broken ankle by a vicious attack of nepotism to the naval salute. Everything else after that year was a violation of her intellectual property and therefore the manufacturers would claim negligence to the courts.

The TM is not just a mark anymore. The person here was an hired mafia assurance to cast the family of legal marriages into a stormy burial with the Titanic. The memorial in that era was made a blessing on this day of remembrance with the protection offering of yellow. Its length was approximately two hundred fourteen centimeters in length and approximately ten centimeters in width. The scarf was in keeping with the military oaths where somebody someday would see its worth in remembrance too. As for the literary characters of the mafia maiden was the Archbishop of York who is catholic. I can only guess that in the Diocese of Ontario, the Anglican counterpart is following the Archbishop of Canterbury. Maybe no one really knows for sure who is who after a decade of Meacham surveys. However, within the trained gallery, there is a plethora of metric versions of concrete pillars to include the number 8864. "The way of righteousness is life and, in the pathway, thereof, there is no death."

There were no regrets to the continued education of the artist to support the ABD. It is a proven merit where it can also mean that we were not self-designated. Azariah means a more perfect understanding of the author's intents and maybe even the ultimate protection against an holy league of pseudo lawyers. Keynesian theories are not monetary and there was too much emphasis placed in the hands of scalpers. The evolution of a system to profit from the development of impossible order was showing the slow poke nuclear reactor to the development of a dirty bomb in our own backyard.

Social justice citations of thermodynamics are not just myth here and the conversion of heat is the construction model used to balance the budget for the political elite. Luckily my leaf was perfectly falling. Just like the umbilical cord. It was supposed to represent value given to the unsigned photograph on the beach of her grandfather's homeland. It was a showing of the ghost which trusted the actions of a government to the betterment of our children. It was unusable land that had never been licensed with mathematical derivatives in statistical mathematics to expose the hospital's arrow of idealized time to either increase or decrease an isolated system.

The Ross Sea is in the Antarctic region where possibly the largest regions of unclaimed territory still exist. Scientists use the area to report information to an insatiable public. In contrast to the Bearing Sea, where everything from Nunavut to the Arctic circle is a projection of the arch vest of the scarf presentation in an archive of Canadian presentations.

There are multiple realty listings which show the North American trend toward an University President. I could not be incorporated with that title. The other obvious sign of integration was the tattoo. A court's system could not just zap these out of their system after a period of ten years of affordable signatories for the belligerent utility of exchanging one limb for another. Science shows us that nothing is faster than the speed of light on earth. Yet in the cosmos, there can be many interpretations of the equation of distance equaling the rate by the time since time in a vacuum may or may not exist. For many an artist, grasping the visual reality of breaking the speed of sound, meant that what was being created should be valuable to the existence of an higher learning model than just one man's riding in the political office of volunteers. The fifth sense in the suspension of gravitational force constants allows the artist to see in three dimensions and not just in mathematical formulas.

One cannot overcome death. However, to exist in an environment that is of pure fiction would be a nightmare, even if it is a real platform in space. There is no colour. There is only light captured in very many forms with the chemical analysis of processes in a value chain of educated minds. To see our bodies in the natural temptation of free fall may sometimes be the safeguard against the protagonist of literary oration. My paintings are produced in the secondary market with a technique which makes the audience think about colour either in music or particles of light here on earth. The record of these results of subject matter lie somewhere between non-fiction and fiction and they are a means of elevation to ward off the Roshis of nuclear attack here in my backyard.

The aviation industry knew exactly how the attacks could be made more accessible through the network of telecommunication's industries. Here the importation of cellular technology allowed many opportunities for sales, yet we do not always see the same results of those technologies for the long-term sustainability to our infrastructure. Transportation industries paid ultimately in the end for the battle between the converging markets. To prove this assumption, Rodney still has a signature imprint on his upper lip with his daughter taking the podium with him, both mocking the Proust in all literary covers.

My Bank Street address to the popular Canada Wood Council and the Doctor of my ABD title is now a corporation which hold suasion power over the individual rights of ownership from a Canadian Constitution. As the title holder of our esteemed Great Seal, my work of original copyright confirms all places of attendance with the secondary confirmation. It refers geographically to shrubs of the rose family of the genus Physocarpus, with showy clusters of white flowers and peeling bark. They are found on the Pacific coast of Canada and along the shores of the Great Lakes. They have reminded me of an exclusive legal right granted for a specific author designer to print, publish, perform, film or record literary, artistic and musical material. Also, as a point of recognition to the house of facts is the sir name Cormier, with an obelisk, who was the architect and engineer that designed the Superior Court of Canada Buildings in Ottawa for which the cornerstone laid is dated to Queen Elizabeth II.

Avant la letter means before the name was coined. Sir Alcock with an obelisk was knighted in 1919 and died in a flying accident in a version of the Victors Vimy aircraft. This is mentioned here for the history of the first non-stop flight across the Atlantic Ocean from Newfoundland to Ireland at a time before Canada had an Attorney General Minister as legal advisor to government. With a title like Major, would you consider working for a Major Baum and would you further record this as a security threat to our cities of Canadian born children where the honours and integrity of our WWI grandfathers would have blessed our children both female and male alike?

The first law of thermodynamics considers that energy cannot be created or destroyed: it can only change from one form to another as from potential to kinetic. Entropy is the measure of disorder and as the case study shows, it is always increasing. We also know as a matter of study is the proof that history does not repeat itself in the core curriculum of operational commitments based in the center block on Parliament Hill as opposed to the White House. The vista here from the architecture is from the War Museum as it captures the framed view from the LaBreton Flats.

Our trust is the obligation of Peace to the contractual obligation of people from Pacific coasts, Arctic oceans and Atlantic air spaces. Personally aligned with these supports is my statement of not wanting my home to be turned into un ville horror of cardinal corporate structures to outweigh the ladder of the ordinal postal codes. If one proposes, the other abstains. Judging from the progression of laws in this country, the ideal situation could be taken as far as the nature of survival which also eliminates the navy component since the Coast Guard provides the same services.

National identity proves that not all persons are predictions of our future growth here in Canada. If I were U in the Julien calendar, the NATO supply would also see the absolute authority of the American people as separated from the Canadian publishing rights of your ABD status. Thankfully, our Administration shows legally that the element of air and land forces are the protections in a mode of transport that is real to the basis of service on behalf of the economic viability extended to the family of military ensigns.

What is the definition of an essential service with an institution of education which does not factor the tax account of our children? When the illiterate is challenged in both official languages, then the believer will construct the sur name not based on military merit. It will be in the capacity of the city and dates of birth to where he is standing today. It was lucky for my situation that the ancillary team in the federal jurisdiction required at least a grade twelve promotion factor.

I am a charm: a colourful soul that is the air between the seas.

CHAPTER NINE

HISTORIES MYTHICAL REALITIES

If I had closed in my hands a set of coins in one and a list of names in the other, which would you choose? There are no right or wrong answers and there are no rewards of keeping these items for your personal protection. Also, why would you even bother to answer the question presented? The point of asking this question is to show that bad things happen to good people, but psychological abuse is a preventable tort in Canadian Law.

So, what is the ultimate bar and who is the one who sets this for a democratic, communist or republican state?

I don't want to over stylize the vulgar in classical literature and neither do I want people to set any more moral iconic images as icons to our tertiary markets of language alphabets. I have only ever wanted the seer to recognize the oak. The ollave is the poet's version of some vision compelling to the dragon which represents a certain type of wisdom. The goddess is not this vision nor or this wisdom. Adam will still be Adam and the invocation of the

Forest Child is the Amethyst of the colour of a still born child named Benjamin.

All these comments are higher levels of the province. They build on the skills of training rather than the paternal lineages of historic religions. If I borrow them, I also must return them; at some point in time. President Kennedy found this out the hard way. Yet, if I am beyond the trespass, then forgiveness is a gift of God alone. Further written is the fact that you are not a failure if this is not possible. Sometimes an hatred can be bigger than any other treaty we can withstand and the idea of having a "Forgiven Soldier" is a promise into your soul as a Canadian.

Maintain an account of your destiny. Hopefully it will not be a rookery of falsified certificates of an Eastir girl's name. The Advent is the word signifying the arrival of something Devine and as our science progresses, sometimes it does not include the word or title of a King. Also note the danger for Eleusis as a translation from Daeira, the daughter of Oceanus, the wise one of the seas, to restore virginity.

Metaphorically, as a rite of renewal to the differences in language and history, the restoration may only be a Band-aid brand. If our policy in monetary terms can replace all items of personal possession, what does it say about the scars on our souls when we realize our government has eclipsed our perfected interests; especially those of our children?

If I knowingly borrowed a culture so vulgar that it would cause death, then I should be corrected for this intent. Yet my K for Kelvin stands for Kindness and it could free our children as a renewable resource. This letter has always led me back to the water's edge where the painting realized a show of lighted celebrations different than the light captured inside our buildings. For us the King is light as stated in my poem. So, without the King, there would be no provision for natural light, and we would be living in darkness. The new testament was supposed to ease our transition of being led into these areas of public office. As for this artist, she believes the investment is the oil painting of the letter K and not the teacher involved with the personality of that same said person. I thought that Tom Thomson did it best for the Canadian public. Yet I don't speak for all groups of artists. To safely and legally replace the command, was to stay invested against crossreferencing the maiden sur name.

The same is not absolute for the case of two males since the elder would have supremacy over the younger and the Passover meal would qualify as the peace offering, like the historic story of Israel. In any case, the freedom to partake of the celebration is a choice you make as a community and family too.

Ms. Tobin is an unwedded mother at a factual point in the social science of vital statistics. Likewise, Ms. Gordon and Ms. Jocko are as well. I am different since I chose not to be an unwedded mother. This is called marketing and as children in a family unit, we learn to do this instinctively where other siblings are there to compete for resources. These women cannot be of the same supported arrangement of marriages to the certificate of ceremonies. One could be classified as a white wedding, for any classification of cultural marriage, while the other lists of people could be free to choose any matter of label as though livestock to the Church or any matter of religious building. Here they leave and enter the markets based on what is capable of being sold and there is nothing international about their political views. This is the basis of my person as a strength to say literally that I don't need or want a Church to make me believe in God. Art here is the beginning of a formal understanding. Here the spiritual respect has connected the law with the law to say that we must abide by the rules of our constitution as opposed to the connection to social services.

To have spiritual respect means that you do not harass a person's personal property and you will have no reason to acquit. If you don't let a pardon go, then when you drown, you will take more than yourself down at the same time.

A bag is symbolic of a type of vessel, different from that which conveys people over water. The contents here are to be protected, kept secret or hidden. The "Captain's Treasure" is the person who realizes that the garden theme was the revealing of the Goddess of Wisdom, Athene. In myth, if cranes were believed to be associated with literary secrets through the observation of flight, then the artist should see the revealing of the rooster as a basis of its resurrection. Holy wisdom is not always a financial instrument and when we are exposed to this understanding throughout our lifetimes, there is an amaranthine beauty in the offer of trust. A sense of peace is achieved with the strategy of a win, win situation.

Science requires a creative process. The X=loch graphically is a calibration of water. There is no vessel other than that which is used to prove it does not exist. Noah would have appreciated the loch for what it was worth as a berthing instead of a title to welcome the casement nimbus.

Art is a good timekeeper without the precision of an atomic clock. Artists also maintain that nobody is decidedly technically more literate than another. Professionally, it would be best for the artist to take a post card over an index card since the attachment leads to a clarification of the word buy and sell for greater autonomy. Poems are merchandise, not speech. Since ink is not the smallest part of the composition either, if compared to a dot, then it really isn't a function of the commerce of letters: that which is secret from that which is public notation. Imagination is the inversion of art, like black is to white.

Secondly, shadows are depictions of symbols of technical expertise. They are totally impersonal. That is something a poet cannot be. Therefore, the Englishman is not a poet at all, but the mathematician in immigration status. Since art is also the study of shadows, the writer becomes a flat, ineffective communicator. He may be expressive, but expression is a psychological form of political will. It is also a preventable abuse. At one point the surrealists tried to bridge the gap between art and artisan with architectural forms, yet the science of art is the study of pure light. The sequence always returns to the arrangement of atmosphere over a legend symbol.

We, as educators should not think Canadian art history belongs with some dyslexic group of old women clinging to the vows of poverty as if they were a continuous revolution of political theory disembodied to feeling guilty about having meaningful relationships within the contractual sense of what is meant to be lawfully wedded.

Killing is not negotiable to people. It is a threat to our security when it comes to the end of a useful life. A cow is a cow. The commerce of a lifetime spent in the industry is from the primary markets of distribution where it has been made safe by our Administration. This is the same for all manner of food for consumption. As a statistical roadblock, the broom closet is no place to store the garden harvests.

Sell what you can and save the rest.

It is my respect as an artist to explore new intellectual materials to conclude analytically that we are not just a social adaptation. In Canada, I see the beauty in the harshness of the shorelines of ice and snow for fishing. They are unrefined materials. Unlike the #04-31332 of the name Masche, written on behalf of the City in the province of Ontario which sees the motto "Your License to Survive" a questionable debate as the two military officials take aim against the Holy Innocents to the driver in question. "And under the wings of justice and wisdom, she will take oaths." The engineer of public commission was a moral insult to the intelligent driver over an empire of male prostitutes.

Grozzelle with an obelisk was a name I prodded to see the competitive athletics of media reporters. Her apoplectic personality of knowing him was like a war in the terminology of medical terms. He is still a mystery on this Father's Day weekend. The medical notation is different than the dentistry model for extreme sports. It is also known that the LGBT community is using these members to increase their politics in the non-profit sector. This might be good for Europe; it is not good for Canada especially with an Imam waiting to be a Ministry of Government agencies. I see my Ninebark as a cultural improvement center for the previous term's leadership. In that legal cause, one house is too much while 144,000 isn't enough. That is the reality of any political party.

The Vanier is becoming obsolete in the embassy addresses of the Balmoral leather in the history of the beginnings of sur names. Yet, despite the schisms involved in the Alexander Pub, St. James Restaurant was the La Grolla, La Petit Restaurant Swiss in Old Quebec City which I hope will be a remembrance for a time when the commission and market of career were not bought or sold like newspapers. Since I have no protection against a litany of torts brought into this country illegally, the brand name Purolator with the first name Ted show just how evil the Enterprise whose Asynchronous Packet of Public Dial ports into the Kingston area is an ITI number or a BPS number. The hackers of the security interests of party leadership knew who and how they obtained their information.

The telephone went dead in my hands.

I tried the cellular phone and it also had no connection. There is no way to contact anyone and it is seen as a threat. It is a threat, first knowing that Black Walnut is used for gunstocks like those of our father's collections of 303s. Tomatoes and apples do not survive near these mature trees. Black varnish is also a very rare building material. The economic scarcity of these building materials are also known by other elite members of the architectural society of Ontario. In the past, it only took one bullet to be a man. Today, in Canada, we are a military for the Government which also includes the respect we have for women to the Crown. The Honourable Justice S. Goffin-Boyd of Ontario was wrong to accuse the author of criminal intent. I wrote a poem to remember the visit into Quebec with the purchase of "Anticoste." He doesn't know that it was purchased to send a message that we understand the provincial crossing into the City with a bridge. His own siblings, I am sure, would be looking for indemnification the same way this Jewish daughter witnessed Yitzhak Rabin as never having celebrated Christmas and so the basis of a schism will always be a thorn in the Lions of Quebec. Statistically here, Judah and Micah, are not the Kings of England and I owe them no special favors for the marriage of MPs from immigrations outside the performance of our CD titles.

Now is the moment of indoctrination to the scarcity of resources as one realizes that war is a defenseless mechanism of rutting seasons. This is what happens when we don't understand our economy well enough to show legally that we do not owe these amnesty persons anything of our provinces of birth. For the father who curses the wife with the words, "The best part of you ran down your mother's legs.", is a report from the ashes of an event from which all children would be innocent. After hearing about these impassioned words, I realized that this was an insult to the man himself and so his fatherhood was stricken from the lands of which taxes were paid. There could be no connection linguistically or literally to this Newfoundland overbearing fascist statement. It has made things very difficult for the Halifax Citadel.

I did train for war initially, however the management of people and resources were a better investment in the persons attached to their innocent earnings against a nation of mysos fathers. Admittedly, I was angry at this religious use of charging our women and abusing the social insurance number system this way by all lawyers within the brand name Ford for Ontario. The entrapment of confidentiality to psychological nuclear intelligence around military occupational codes means that the blood must be on somebody's hands at the end of the day.

There is no blood on my hands and so the bruises inflicted by these privy duty councils of arranged marriages is a Smith to the office of retail sales where the reputation of the artist is in command of the truth. She said she would write it when the ankle was broken where her oath maintained that she could not speak about the Chevrolet brand of the driver who ran them down on the 10 November. The certificate of achievement was completed in 1995. It was an incredible undertaking to the preface of the Cidillia character.

Helen was involved in the Administration of the Union of Public Employees which begat this whole misalignment of people to our children in their future. The A5 was a concept used as a point on the elevation plans of a real piece of property ownership. They could not take that away from her lineages with the families of lower courts. That is why the oil paintings with her signatures are a cover design as well. It proves her designs along with the enrollment as a military member.

Brian took his training after my honour's graduation. I am still waiting for the card of thanks to his daughter's wedding which was scarcely attended by anyone except for the lineage of the family bible. The premise of Law and Conscience to the French language university makes the extremism of our Ottawa Administration to the Holland Gerretsen seem like the attack to push a female off the sidewalk was political and thus the local police, when called, did nothing at all. When the motorcycle was stolen, the local police did nothing at all. When utilities workers blocked off her driveway, she told them to move and apparently, we as taxpayers are not allowed to tell these unionized employees that they are creating a safety infraction of entrapments. For all this I ask the people of rural Canada, when we are protecting the most vulnerable of military ownerships, "Is an unjust law really law?"

A divorce is not the same thing as having no legal recourse. Thus, if you are not married, then you have no family or in-law protection from the lands of which you own. Thus, I did what I could to protect the most vulnerable as a matter of the conditions of putting our children onto the streets of Ontario as though they were characters of old testament misfortunes. As a condition of remembrance, I read those stories in the province of Quebec. Later in my career, Robert and Jennifer, for the record of reported decisions of an hospital ambulance driver, was the father Mark. To that end, my painting was titled not towards the non-profit category of vehicles detailed to the ECCs and CFRs but it was appropriately considering the insurance of the victim of a M.R. as the V.C. to a final judge that also claims his certificates of authentication to the home riding of St. John's, NL in our tax scams of ONT agents.

This may still not matter very much to the clergy that I had read every book studied in a professional program besides being an honours graduate from PE to the truth of how and when the ankle was broken. The proof to myself first of those conditions of hatred will not be forgiven for the false accusations against the soul of the person named Kimberly A. with the CD. The proof of my address here in Ontario is not 705 Division Street. It is found on page 4 of the ISBN 0-13-523895-1 of the Canada Cataloguing in Publication Data number for the year 1991. Furthermore, it has been paid in Canadian currency that was four years before the completion of the banking institute's use of business students from China. As a military member, the secondary insight into a finished good was not the industrial zoning of military engineers to the card of intent by Steve of the TD Monk of the St. Lawrence aesthetic with the names of the Pope Road followers over time.

Elaine is not a boy's name. Nor is Lacey. Yet the first name Kim is exchangeable for both genders as was the name of her spouse. This commonality of diction for the encouragement of the LGBT community has led to the children of provincial addresses a threat to every military occupant of accommodation across Canada to misrepresentation. With the use of the word Missy instead of the titled occupants of residences as Mr. or Mrs. or even MS to the importation of brand name vehicles of licensed drivers is the situation for the title painting "japan." A copy of this has been circulated to prove that there is one and only one marriage to the CDs of Kimberly and Terence.

QEII hospital in Halifax, for the record department of vital statistics should now see the difference between how our government treats widows differently than that of a widower. The oil painting author has signing authority within the legal status of her career over the entrapment incumbent of the physical exam between the sexes of Base Commander screenings for deployment into a theatre of war. The threat to all Canadians from that bidding was not just an hypothetical threat to the protection of freedoms to acknowledge the ability to speak on my own behalf and to act on motions of privilege within the Department responsible for grants to the consulting of the the man only. It was an unfair entrapment of the full moonscape and the MC as opposed to MAC.

Trying to make military women infit to wear the uniform is dictatorial to offences that have no academic certification. The police were told about the threat to our safety and security. The dumping of a Seaking helicopter is not a financial obligation to the sons of our oaths nor was the dumping of the Nimrod into Lake Ontario. It was a planned event by the Land Forces as they formally moved into a separation of grants to the Faculty of Law to zoning regulations and titled change of command parades that are not made publicly known. The family accountant to the Woodside name was fired for the move into New Brunswick and the Chamber of Commerce solicitation was fired for that exact same reason; drug investment is not an investment in our future as the titled author of our land and leadership.

Images of social justice operations of historic properties in Kingston and the Islands clash with the operations of engineers designing bridges.

The first was this metrical story
A fabled terrestrial epigram
Stored between a frosted footprint
In a cosmos of miniature hands
He was a strange poet invested The apostrophe of illusive spaces Spiritually active like a tree.

After that came the gargoyle of vocals
Brothels of a starving conscious Zen
With broad illusions of standard prose
Unjust censures o turbulent blends
Amorally tossed with mirrors to recite
Words spoken in boundary halls Denigrating nuances into a Vanguard of silhouettes.

CHAPTER TEN

ASSIGNMENTS COMPLETED AS REGULATIONS

There is no common law action for infringement of copyright. We are and have never been in a common law situation. Therefore, if one is legally married, there is the no tax burden to offer the nee people of our marriage licenses. The province of Ontario has ruthlessly administered against a lady's first name formally distanced from the nee name with Canadian Forces Decorations of certificates of service to secretly mar the name with the ownership of Churches.

B. is the abbreviation of the call sign to be protected. It is a security to the individual lists of Federal reports. It has a long history attached to the Baron. I stayed the courses of accomplishment to this sacrosanct intrusion of the security of personal property at the Public School for the Ministry of Education from which I was elected to speak. From that experience, it was a clear mandate of these trustees to initiate the fear factor for their conditions of nuclear attack with the Snowbledon name as though it were the name Hitler.

The point to survey here is adequately substantiated in the fact that there is no such use of the punctuation mark or symbol used by an editor to which apportions the use of an arrow to be in conflict with the mathematical use of the greater than and less than entry into the conflict resolution of connecting minute details of our leadership to a public debate. Clearly the name Disraeli, in relation to the Queen's library of reserve personnel must have known that I would condition my own security from the absit omen. The number was exchanged, not lost, to protect both paternal and maternal parents. For those not as well prepared for the Defence, I have the right to speak on my own behalf. I went to Ottawa and I wrote to the Senate about the attempts of identity theft here in the Limestone City.

I claim with copyright both the written and electronic versions of my registrations here for which one is a lullaby for the Federal Courts in the Province of Ontario. I am the Vice in a sport for which we support our interests in the forest child. It is also the environment where the K is for kindness that cannot be exchanged for an exorcism of the Mormon confession.

The confession is a soiling of every event that we carefully journaled since 1978. The yearbook has my name on it. The IBM computer holding tax man by the name of Crastina was the most discourteously sent agent of Canada that was ever encountered until we met with Constable Bradshaw. To have doubted my truth beyond a reasonable doubt and to further Mar the person with the April month of an abuse so great that not even my own mother could forgive. Just remember that what goes around will also come around to you.

I worked for the rights of my public title to the Prime Minister of Canada and not the Imam of the Shoppers

Drug Mart employee called my sister. To that end I have no attachment to the title of a President of statutes to the Brotherhood of Electrical Workers where I have sited the Senator Segal in the marketplace behind City Hall. For me the CGal abbreviation of the name was the reminder of a vessel used to hold contents of the Garnishment Act and my kab is the vessel used to hold dry goods. Thinking outside the box is the Gaming Act which has been used with the aid of the Yuan currency. Profiles of both the Gaming Act and the Garnishment Act are proofs of the entrapment in the penitentiary land where a credit card company can garnishee 20 % of net wages, CPP, and EI and then a judge can increase or decrease the amount of garnishments. By providing the truth to the entrapments set up by Constable Bradshaw and further directed to the holder of the tax account by non-profit religious hospitals and to the stealing of her "good works" of art in exchange for the D'hart progression is a form of civil law corruption by protecting Gay Pride entrapments for unionized employment.

There is a connection statistically between those unwed mothers in their social agenda in comparison to the polygamist cult. The condition of an unwed father to the Pope, has a mother as though she were the first Eve of biblical relations. This is academically unfair to those with long term interests in the businesses in Canada as markets. Eventually, like the nursing profession, they will move south of the border in order to realize a higher rate of return on their skills. Hospitals do not produce finished goods, yet they do have retail space rented out to the public that sells and is profitable for the venue to which goodwill may be supported.

My gallery is not there and so the current competition is a slander to the taxpayer at intestate for her last will and not the Gaming Act or the Garnishment Act of the financial institution for filing our taxes every year. I was not born in Exeter, Ontario and the assurance of that location is not a part of where my children would ever be connected either maternally or linguistically. Thus, the insurance of being trained for employment in the industrial capacity shows how the volunteer membership at the venues in hospitals does not help with the economic viability of our country where the role of command is navigation and safety. The role of communication is traffic. The business of a director better realizes the ability of the capacity to move and continue without having to declare bankruptcy.

My tax account is just that and it should not be manipulated by 40,000 employees across all provinces who do not have proof of a sworn oath to the Government of Canada. From that certificate, I have never given anyone any reason to publicly haze myself or my children the way we have been inflicted with hatreds so unworthy of the dignity of one human being to another as has been done by MR Holland and Mr. Downes since 1996 which is four years before the present Mayor of 2000.

I realized at the time of arrival to that requested message in organizational structure, that the best way to go around the situation was to beholden to the academic advancement in the most appropriate time and place possible. Our health cards also did not have to lead to a hole of the rectal examination to begrudge the possession of a military uniform to say the hospital greens. In contrast to my blue uniform and to my parenting skills, what was learned from the endurance in the persistence in memory of our landscapes was the belief that the soldier could overcome death. To that belief, I can't answer for other more accomplished artists. They may be following a different cost account to the publishers of Penguin geographical connections.

The ghost in this house didn't choose that author of "Remembrance of Things Past" though. In terms of publishing rights, it wasn't a very prolific choice for the other non-fiction status publications on that same shelf. Regarding its placement, it was situated forth from the right where there were two other non-fiction books whose Oxford publishers were well established by the time I was registered in the public primary school system. Everything else on the shelf was an academic study of the professional designation of mathematics, accounting, biology, chemistry, and the economics of the theory of statistics. The significance of the law was a deliberate 19 from the left for the chronicled date of the D-Day invasion at Normandy, France.

Even if I had some type of relapse in my memory to recall this book being placed on the floor that morning, what are the odds that it would coincide with my spouse's hockey jersey number, the house number of my utility account and its number being the same as my sister's utility account! I thought this was more than just statistical coincidence, so it had to be documented as a lineage since the Second World War here in Canadian taxation.

Today, it doesn't really matter as to whether you believe this story of what pops out at you to capture your attention for an unwanted solicitation but it should matter to you to understand the vulgarity in intimidation to the non-compos status of soldiers with the Maple Leaf. When I wrote that there were terrorists with attitudes of assassins, I was well within my authority to do so on behalf of all other innocent families of military status.

The local police were not going to muster themselves for our benefit. They had too much debt taking care of the penitentiary legalities of their number system to calculate correctly the lady of Longfellow's Evangeline of the frostbitten druids. I too may be holding some important letters that could prove your entrapments as harassment and abuse of authority to lands which you do not own.

The creation of "Parks n' Picnics" was a commission to the Redmond Realty. I had no problem realizing that the requested occupants with the capacity to hire was for a child with the same first name. Keirstead is a sur name whose works are purchased on a regular basis, however what I didn't know was that he was a former local police officer. The fact that police stick together, shows the favoritism toward this individual's property and how the hatred to my taxation account could be manipulated by the City of Kingston using vehicle accounting systems in the Province of Ontario with the vehicles used for transporting criminals around the City.

My knowledge of military codes to CFRs and ECCs for the operations of our Maple Leaf ensign could be similar, but not the same. The name to quote here is a David to the Benjamin of a stillborn baby whose parents moved forward by making the trip to Toronto, Ontario to prove their parenting skills with two more siblings. How often does this happen in the order of despatchers of the local police?

A painting style cannot be plagiarized as a building can like the Twin Towers. So whether or not you are involved in a struggle of competition, then make sure you stand up to the fraud with the geometry of your space by telling this ghost story and make the world believe in what it is that the Old Bill used to Arc the security of his Joan to my daughter at the request of the penitentiary attorney general's staff to entrap the artist of the number 19 years of age to the assumption of blood alcohol limits with licenses to drive before the age of 21.

I knew too much of the artisan's lingo to let the slander of my name sake go into delivering just any old child out of bondage. The third in line to the initials KB used her middle initial G. So, the motivation to use a sign on her property in the middle C signature was made real to the banking institution as proof between the mediators of heaven and earth about his ability to read music.

The Mrs. on this signing authority is a civilized person who would not allow some insane emasculated vasectomy driven population of LGBT proclamations with gender issues to control the sculptress. None of us can go back to the womb of blood money to the record of adoptions. A good business manager would not allow this to happen.

Kandinsky was a pioneer in abstract art or so the story of art concludes. From early twentieth century origins, he could also be described as a Christian who worked the apocalyptic imagery in curvilinear form. Both he and Salvador Dali were the technical writers of the new formal components of light and colour. It is from these new forms of expression that the artist can differentiate language from communication or that which is speech. Even more vivid in historical classification, was the evolution of transferring imagery from the thirteenth century cathedrals onto panels or easels. That was a moment of freedom from a strict religious sect. Even further into the psyche of constitutional law and freedoms, is the fact that if one area falls into chaos, everybody will want to exert some force on the action. The Liberal concert hall of Jesuit nuns and priests projected their own Queen's University debate to the legality of party persuasions for Canadians by purposely destroying other people's historic property in the downtown. It wasn't just exclusive to the business sector either. It also extended into the children of our Social Insurance Number systems. From those rights of visitations, as though they too were ghosts to the utilities of ownership to the holiday season called Christmas, was the Corporation of pharmaceuticals in the food chain. This was strictly a mathematical expression to legally order illiterate women to be committed to the health care system through Government issued Health Cards and Driver's Licenses to enhance the legalization and use of marijuana in opposition to our military standards of absolute abstinence in the workplace. Power here meant for the most part that tax collectors would be off the hook if there were issues with the compensation for vehicle write-offs and to protect absolutely the namesake of police units with the brand name Ford.

Hayes is the sur name for an optometrist. I expect she is now retired with an accomplishment of patients to have, whether upgraded with the latest technology or not, the ability to help people see better. The accomplishment of a professional designation to the Doctor of Optometry as opposed to the Doctor of Letters is the classic education to either a win, win; win, lose; or lose, lose situation. We, as consumers to public stations, have never differentiated the need of one physician over another until we see that, due to the differences in languages of our populations in Canadian cities, that now Canadians have no proper representation either for health care or for security of our personal property since the classic education may be like those of a Russian composer that has been provided with his education on the world stage by the interests of the communist state. Catherine of Alexandria tried to portray a different result to these dangers involving powerful institutions and she too ended up a detail fixed in the stone mason's archives of compartmentalization.

Within the commission of technical services for the safe use of our appliances, the functionality of building materials was not so readily demanding to the homeowner. They were however calculated risks for the insurance industry to the amount of fires or renovations that would be required of the replacement value to the occupants. If the local police were tampering with those ownership privileges by contracting to other provinces to eliminate the intelligence of the occupational rights by institutional officer Imams or MCs to the handcuff and shackles used to destroy the faith in our leadership of community, then Bonnard would not be seen as a great master. Yet, he like this artist saw the real value in light and he would capture the best perceptions of ancient light. To some people, this may seem a primitive skill. I tended to view the approach to art overall as an economically safe mechanism of survival in a world of scarce resources. If one must see much of this world from ancient light, then the motivation to hold as much of that knowledge as you can, should also require the best representation of thoughts within a painting as you can possibly do for the mobility of an even bigger representation of the world.

The name Marie was painted on his canvas. Mon Marie is an image in the window of light to a word surmounted into a personal collection of memories as if she would remain in that light forever. She is above the crowed city below and the view onto our Canadian landscapes here at the letter of middle C is vivid and rich in tone and accent. Here our country is not a church to fight over.

In our northern climates, we can be in darkness for as much as six months of a calendar year. The identity of the people is not so much a limitation to their growth potential as it is to their lack of noise. Visually adept, sculpture is what Giotto was to the painted "Nativity" back in the thirteenth century. To us, it wasn't important enough to depict the urban theme in inactive states. It was important to use everything efficiently as with the whaling season and the appreciation of light to be nature's gift of intervention. We understand it.

I anticipate the export of these ideas as personal property.

Furthermore, it is not solicitation. It is communication and traffic in the exchange of ideas, and it embodies the treaties of old surveys. Here both memberships of parents are radiant. The whole process of life is beautiful once we, who are married, realize it too is a protection for which we owe nobody. Can we untangle the forest of innovation by changing the way we view our resources? There can be no other eternity for Canada than when we are logistically protected by the occupational titles of ownership.

The sculpture that has no expression is still an accomplishment. The order is without parasites. It is an entire life force with the possibility of an universe in the stone or bone for which the artist has composed with just one single word. The formality is enhanced by the soul of nature. It is thick and Inuktuk. It gives everything it embraces to the audience, even like a mirror which brings the vastness of the oceans to another couplet of civilizations. Objective inventiveness is an estranged vanity of words, smells, hearing, feeling and touching of another dimension within the plane of existence of lost time. Without this exposure of sculpture, I sense I would see much less of my Canada. The connection to the soldier and ensign now one. It is a special municipality from which there is respect for the earnest transmission and livelihoods of impressions from atop of the world.

So where do we go from here?

Certainly, it won't be back to our children nor they to us. We must all speak for ourselves for no person should have to assume the identity of another. In this modern age of art and design, we are prudent to becoming stand-alone instruments. Some, sadly, are becoming an endangered species with mechanical difficulties as though there is a vision of language modeled inside an electric circuit on a pedestal of grammar from its etymological bearings. She will vanish out of sight if we don't appreciate the works as a collective agreement.

CHAPTER ELEVEN

EMPIRES GOWAN DRAGONS

Without surviving issue is what they have come to represent. While as children of the apprentice, there may have been noticed a preference to favor one hand over the other. It was soon discovered that the mobility of the canvas with its awkward proportions, required the artist to work the paint into a story to tell the world. Besides that, every colour used was different in texture so the design was like they were boughten from different elements of the earth. Escher too had learned to use his vision of curved perspectives as a foundation outside the philosophy of geometry. The sir name Barker is still associated here with curvilinear panoramic landscapes and physiological space.

A pin was given to her keeping by the RCMP. It was the illustration of the province of Saskatchewan. Its royal lineage was traced back to the Royal Visit of Princess Margaret, the sister of Queen Elizabeth II. At another point in her career, she was given a trinket representing the Royal Dragoons, the troops of which were thought to have been a force of breathing fire. Unsure of what to do with the artifacts, since they were outside the myth of pictorial landscapes, she believed in all likelihood that the roll of a combat soldier needed to have closure and so she was selected to compare its regency with the observation of the deceased from an accident on Granville Street in her home town. She, being the newly crowned governess to the meteor of a British Royal was attentive to its spiritual connotations of a peaceful future condition for all peoples.

As she sketched the landscapes of her Canadian ensign, for her the commissioning illustration, the dragoon badge was kept secret from her Redmond commission. She did remember that he requested to have his grandchildren painted into the setting and that some flowers should be placed along the path leading to the marina landing. She recalled that producing those on sight sketches were the easiest aspects of the request without the use of graph paper. The most difficult was the colours to represent the highlights set inside the grassy knoll which led into the Depot Lakes. The use of daisies for the Gowan use of yellow and white were a connection to the presentation with the city of Ottawa and its peoples.

A Gowan is the Scottish term for any white or yellow field flower with its colour relational to gold ores. The Barker who first claimed that system of curvilinear theory did so around 1819 using only mathematical perspectives. At the time, she employed his theory against the rigid influences of linear geometry. Linear or graphic art, it was argued, was more influential to the advancement of structural employment in architecture. Yet, in connection with the human eye for the landscape perspectives to plot the achievement of a house, we had to integrate the grounding of influences.

Integrating a more investigative approach to the military pattern to complete the study of art and its colours associated with the Canadian landscape showed the potential which treated pigments like a compromise between the straight conformists and the unified language. Her sketches were the basis for calculations used in the enlightenment of the postings where the discovery of time and space proves to an assonant that ghosts cannot be nailed to the cross.

The leader must stand. Seek means interchange. Towns and cities mean the difference between didactic verses elenchus. The aporia of the appellation to the Caledonian of the invented art is not a matter of brain over brawn. It was like an obedience to the security without the dwelling or weaponry used for the insanity of battles fought. There is always an understanding in the generations of artistic research.

We were so often confronted with challenges as to the validity of cowardly gossiping that a new work of art, Canadian art, was a subject that even the highest titled uniform could not overlook. The subject was always something worth appreciating. I started with the name Yttriyanta for its literary beginnings. Everything was totally fiction. Then once the name catches in the mind, it metamorphosis as it passes through the wind, beyond the trees and along the ground. The only rule maintained was that you are never, ever allowed to touch the subject. Use brushes, carving tools or whatever means you have at your disposal to capture the essence of what is happening before your eyes: lose the perspective of interpretation.

This is the essence of curvilinear theory. The method chosen for presentation meant that nobody was ever going to tell me that it didn't exist and instead of doing workshops for the public gathering, I became a leader in truth to say artists are hunters and gathers of light. In the essence of education, that is what the student strives for ultimately. In truth, the theory of what she saw and the freedom to express may just as easily have been found to exist in a gallery of trees along the Canada trail or centered in the middle of a street scene on a snowy winter's day. My vision of the landscapes even has been a securely hidden subject inside a piece of literature. Yet, the formidable point to disclose about elementary particles with those thermodynamic energy calculations, is to make sure not to distort the light in progression of the opportunity to practice the details.

I don't believe in the demanding persistence of ghosts. In the case of military personnel, since giving signing authority over to government, as in a prior form to a legal will, then mistakes can be used as the case study shown between the Rose VS. Pim (1953) interpretation to the mistake of complete agreement.

The Past President of the club presented this situation for the allocation of risk between the local police and the degrees held by the board. In terms of the inequality to time in uniform to the distribution of our taxes, then how is the court going to see the difference between life and liberty in a peaceful progression? The government, not the contract between airline industry providers, are aware of the provisions given to the many departures of air flights with engineers, not stewardesses to secure the manuscripts of our existence within the pay scale to a CPP. There can be loss of property if there is a loss of identity to title the works against the title of the artist. Wendy's statement was a misrepresentation as a foster parent which caused the exasperation and escalated aggressions to turn the whole community into a gulag of our military titles against those of the civilian community. Otis Tamasauskas did the same thing for the BHFA Class of 2010 in Ontario Hall open house convocation. I don't think I could handle that child's death "One More Time With Feeling." At the master's level of training standards, it seemed to provide us for a level of art which turns our Administration into a downward spiral as life shifts into language AI technology instead.

My son was given a cow. To the hoax, I will stand against that solicitation of penitentiary duty with the belief that light is both wave and particle theory. That would be indisputable. As for the science in that list of TD bursaries advertising St. Lawrence College, where did you expect to sell those write-offs? I guess my advice is to beware of where you drop off your cookies since an active intervention may be running in the background of another employee's account using your postal code for its drop-off. The security is knowing that the poetry written for O Canada bears the titled name Weir.

That knowledge came from a hymn book that was long forgotten. It was given to her like the Dragoon hat badge. Maybe someday she will return its adjutant sponsorship throughout our emersion with the CD Medal of Honour to Canada. As parents, we both have paid the fines for the rank and file unknown soldier: addendum material for the Cadet corporation. I have, as a privilege to drive, transported the spirits elsewhere in the cosmos where we cannot industrialize their landscapes.

The sword is an honourable mention for the truth. The sur name Rybca is a truth to the threat of commerce comparing the occult with the Onyx pen usage for making persons responsible for signatures even though they were not a party to the conditions of the contracts undertaken by other similar institutions and family gravesites. That was the point where she put a stop to the promotion of a formidable import into Canada at their immediate family's expense. Her sister took away the peaceful progression into the future with the New Year of her birthday. A sad moment for our siblings. Yet, she doesn't have a Captain for every month. The title commissioned for the saving of the faith was "The Calendar Year." It was unknown to them at the municipality of my parents and it was considered for the tort before the infraction of identity theft that took place. It will say that you will not walk away from the artist who smiled at her only daughter at convocation from among the thousands of graduates that year. The cost of doing business for the exchange of commerce was the loss of an equal opportunity to compete in the same province of her birth.

The term atelier is French. The odds were eight to three to correct the translation of Naples yellow before my sister will ever get away with a plea of innocence to the offer of doubling my money. There is a caveat which states there is an issue of safety first and our uniforms were not a function of the stock market. At the club, the loss of the dish to hold a few morsels of food while tending their flock means that you inflicted the injustice of her safety in the signing for expenses that were contracted by license of trademark. Real or otherwise denoted, we have all met the Commissars of both RMC and Queen's faculty and that certainly was not for nothing. We did not volunteer for that! My uniform will not be soiled for that supply retinue attributable for its membership.

It is a Canadian holding secret letters. The AI of first persons in the collection of names to her art collection may be something familiar to the Elohim. I say this since it was Captain Gower who gave our listings to the MLS. Likewise, the wife of my Captain used the resources of the Administration to contract our SISIP lineages into a subdivision legal infraction from the Personal Insurance Company AR132/78 as I remembered the 04 report of the accident on Counter Street.

In another area of bidding for property as I saw him walking towards us, his facial expression bidding our attendance at the event was one of enlightened notoriety. He took placement at the head of the table and opened his hands to reveal a puppy. As part of the Administrator's experience, it was my job to authenticate the records on premises for security purposes. Very quickly though, before I could reach up and grab the animal, he passed his possession on to the next person sitting next to him. I was very spiteful of this mischief and I asked, "Is that a newborn?" He didn't answer but motioned instead for me to watch as the animal was handled by every person at the table. I was the last to receive the tiny bundle of wet fur. I felt envious though and when the little boy took the puppy from me before I even had a chance to certain its identity: I looked down. Exposed there in my hands were the internal organs of the bottom half of the animal, all glued and squishy.

I screamed for this is what it felt like to be posted into that City. I knew it was just a joke, but the emotion of horror was so great what else was there for me to do.

CHAPTER TWELVE

WINGS EXPOSING FOLLY

The urban legend is not always a rite of passage. Guilt by association to the dead poet's society is a derogatory assent for the chain of Newfoundland bars in the old port of St. John's CRA account. The charitable cause for this is long past the Florenceville of New Brunswick in a standard of origin to the displaced shadow of a legacy to the endless supply of comments about blood being thicker than water.

She used her first name Terry to the Kennedy name offensive by consensus to the assignation of a President of the United States. Her company placement of widows before widowers and vice-versa to the file of ancestry DNA before there ever was a LGBT community. Here it must be made explicit that hysterectomies are not substitutes for the law of asylum seekers here in this City. Ivy 67 is the character that means two objects cannot occupy the same space at the same time. Therefore, the Master could not be ranked with the Master. Logistics here was never an affiliate of the government department for dumping a party candidate upholding the stand on social justice for children who don't know or even care about the absolute parental investment. Local police had no right to access the military portfolio to condemn the ownership of women to their driveways. I was the one who returned the aircraft wreckage from Norfolk, VA. The loss of my security from the Canadian Border Services agents on the return knew they would also have access to the parental obligation of my spouse while I was away on temporary duty – TD. They sacrificed the sanity of my property with the charitable causes of Toronto's elite pride parades over and above the Christmas festival for families with their children.

It is important in contract law to substantiate the grounds in which a contract may be impeached. Here the term Peach is used for the brother of Nina in the capacity of the military community to protect his commission at the expense of mine. If lands were bought for the purposes of government contracts, then compensation could be awarded if these same contracts were cancelled. In the newest version of Rose VS Pim, there was no condition from which to rectify the negotiations as the government was not a party to the negotiations for Rose and in the instruction of texts, there was no agreement to the terms accepting the posting of wages to the lease/rental agreements. The fact that the name Saunders had access to military programming data over the survey legends of Federal reserves meant that the legal status of support for the condition of contract to a cost performance in labor for the aircraft shows that the artist sent was a form of hysteresis in the form of programmable personal dependents to Federal taxation. This term when applied to the economics of situations in which one party refuses to return to the original agreement due to the fact it would receive a greater benefit from the breach of performance than could be gained by full performance.

The past knowledge of secret clearances for job postings due to an obelisk of events leading to the space shuttle Challenger were miniscule in 1986 if compared with the loss of democracy for shifts in manufacturing and zoning traffic by-laws within the City of Toronto. This was also the connection she had been seeking with the fact that she was dismally puzzled about why her vehicle was written off so quietly by the insurance agents of that same stated City. At that same moment of actualization, the approach of her was seen from the construction of a cathedral in a dream while overlooking the waters below. She wasn't a shadow but was placed there to protect from the bombs that might fall against the British Isles.

She was dressed in tee shirt and jeans which seemed to fit the dress code of the other members working for the same cause. There was a crane available to secure the scaffolding and she gave the order to hoist the ladder for placement along the spire so that the very tip of the steeple could be reached. All worked ceased at that moment when she realized the event was a divine moment to the use of the female gender in association with the spire of this historic site. Like the women on Mount Rushmore who had campaigned for their rights of justice and equality, she ascended the ladder to capture the view of the waters below.

She wrote: Femininity is like a voided space. Shadows are its single blessing. Corners between two walls where wood meets wood.

Shadows of a secret stronger than sound and lighter than death.

The epiphany of those words from a dream where glimpses of something foreign is something to look forward to, it was probably more important than knowing our parental lineages.

If the world had suddenly stopped turning at that very moment, the defendants could not be classified as both parties at the same time and the failure to comply with the specific performance of the repair to any motor vehicle would have placed the Ministry in the situation of contempt for her as opposed to him. If with child, the courts could not grant an equitable remedy against infant defendants. I was the driver in a vehicle accident with my son as witness and was also the pedestrian who had escaped death so many years ago. The fact that I was the female driver is the most important issue to establish and I get goose bumps every time I recall this accident. If in the case that the driver was a male, it would be impossible to make a decision of contract due to it becoming voidable at their truth of the accident number not being their fault as opposed to the City trying to access the Garnishment of her wages Act. As a matter of insistence of symmetry, it was hardly fair to the injured victim to insist to her spouse that it was not her fault. Even with the authority of her son as witness, her remedy was denied by local police with an agenda.

This is the second time the courts have used the military to place the lives of innocent parties in peril. In both circumstances, the female grammatical gender has been rescinded instead of completed as the work on a house identity is never fully completed. The land, over and above the construction model of building and equipment, is the value of the artist herself.

If the plaintiff can prove absolutely that both the genders are not theirs, then the condition of Quantum Merit or expectations are not valid as the Cohr's of 411 College Street have tried to condition for contract without the leverage of an architectural firm as opposed to the postal address of Peter N.

As a reputable party, there can be no execution order given to sell various chattels after an appropriate period of grace if those persons were fired before the agent was liable apart from the contract. In this case Saunders went ahead with the principal for the purposes of obtaining goods on credit at the expense of the ownership title to the land as an asset of the artist. Here the name Cannon would apply to the real title when the principal becomes bankrupt or insane or dies. That is what Constable Bradshaw was trying to establish in order to criminalize the actual title holder to her tax account.

In the situation of trust to the Rose clan as a Rose of duel identity, only the threat of a breach of a warranty could be sited for a valid claim to the address since the agent and principal are assured of the continued well-being of the owner and designer over and above the Reverend Pastor Needham for bastardizing their lineages of church records.

If I had considered the offer made by Peter, it would have been terminated in the courts anyway as a condition of an employment relationship which causes the performance to be an engineered sequence of never-ending agreements and thus an impossible performance.

Let's not forget! Lest we forget the Administration of the Federal Courts system, the third party may be liable for negligent representation as a Doe. Jane in this case sees the Cavanaugh of medical practice to bias its employment of physicians from within the survey of Baron titles for all military and civilian postings that would have status for school bus drivers. As owners of titles, we just needed to establish how different that sexual predator was to the infantry of common law armories.

This is not exactly what I would call an agreement when posting season arrives and we are entrapped by the selling agents of realty brokerages with the messages sent by Ottawa. The clan is a different organizational structure of strategic management and it should not be considered a family business. It is all about paying for information to take you up the next steps of the corporate ladder. The constituency speaker Milliken should not have allowed the provincial courts to enter the confidential subject material of F-18 aircraft maintenance to sell to the Vietnamese for a school instructing aeronautics. The subject could be sabotage. The office has intentionally used real estate as an entry into criminal codes and common law courts to involve IBM programmers to discharge the legal contracts of military college associate professors with the titled Mayor and then to follow through with the garnishment of wages to the female officers of their personal ownership of undergarments with the display of sanitary products.

In the domain of intellectual property infringement, the use of provincial courts to access an owner's trademark to sell and enforce judgements against the legally licensed driver to her son's attendance at college by a personal vehicle, not public transit, is a strict violation of their ownership to education. It is a form of communism and is a tort across all Canada especially when we have distance education. While although it is a risky certification, it is better than having your children bastardized by the political elite of any one or all the political leaderships to voters in social media platforms.

The people deliberately pursuing these types of conflicts of interest when it comes to landing a perfect job, whether the trademark is registered or not, are a form of blackmail from section 7 of the Intellectual Property Act. As for Goodes Hall and the unused buildings of Victorian era properties cheaply available to redesign and upgrade to meet Canadian Building Code efficiencies of building materials has not significantly proven that the new is better than the old Bill.

Then the telephone landline to psychologically impose import taxes on our trading partners in order to achieve this level of sabotage to ownership shows how cellular emergency notification can be just as corrupt a communication service as are the social votes for organizational likes from Twitter or Facebook followers. The Vocational KCVI graduates were dispersed by the MPP from Holland and when the parents get involved with their expertise of architectural knowledge, Queen's University and the legal representation of the Department of Engineering allows Escheat to Trump the sexual degradation of all women in the workplace. In the system of merger to European descent with our Canadian images I give the essence of undue influences of harassment to our business ownership without the father as a founder to nickel and dime with Parks Canada and the month of March. On the other hand, the hospitalization of cancer patients is involving the American Administration into our health care agenda. To that end, it may be a fact of calculated originality to design your driveway without the aid of municipal by-law enforcement or ambulance service invoices as they seem to never stop harassing the owner to pay more than once for the same invoice.

With an academic profile to honour any business, this would not have been imagined in the wildest dreams of any trophy distress. A military career and my uninterrupted vision of Canada shows a source of leadership of inspiration for many students entering the work force and where we have never been issued an adverse economic condition statement as grounds for dismissal. I see there is no other remedy except for the parents to be reinstated as married before their children were born.

The textbook example of marriage explains the premise of avoiding being executed by grants in duplicate when there is proof of ownership and title to the goods produced without having to go through customs searches every time we are on exercise with the army of other countries. Land is non depreciating, even as a Gowan field worth nothing. As I see the architecture with an existing arrangement for the security of our children in the communities we are invested, the Val and Vincent were discharged from the case of my provincial holdings in 2010.

Lord Dennings with an obelisk is a citation you won't easily find unless you know exactly where to look. If at once it has been found, it might appear that the courts assert the minimization of mistake in the etiquette of buying and selling to finally make the transaction profitable. If there is doubt to the premise of the purchase to the seller, then there is no existence and the remedy to the mistake to return the situation to afford relief when a court considers it unfair or unjust not to correct it where the contract did not exist as their differences to assuming risk were too great to have contemplated a contract in the first place. This is where the polygamist neighbor is a threat to our country.

Land is a title without the interference of a house or vessel to which parties' contractual agreements can be mistaken in a contract that bears risk of a change in the subject matter. The effect of mistake to the selling of land is almost impossible to discharge as an item affecting assumptions. The whole of five hundred yards is substantial if the logo or trademark is abused by foreign investors from these religious cults. As a negotiable instrument to the insurance and further into the changeover of covenants to the spires that are all over sixty feet high, the steradian error and omission is more than 4mm.

Valley of Snow

Reaching endless song.
Dare to stand!
Whisper of Winged fathers,
Their migrant sands;
Alone to enchant,
Scented portions,
Breathing garden,
Snow in ebony black.
Cling to thy land
Shining in yesterday's valley.
Designs of spiritual plan.
Striving to improve
Imperfect grains of fame;
Girlfriends felling,
White rye moats.
Valley of snow
In a land of hope.

Mercantile quality does not have the same provision of implied terminology as all the clauses within the Sale of Goods Act. It is believed that the courts assume delivery and payment are concurrent conditions and that the transaction is presumed to be a cash sale. In the event of nonpayment, a seller may insist on a term entitling it to take possession in the event of nonpayment. In the formal ownership of land and tenants, the difference between a sale and the contract of quality to the condition of a sale is the condition within an action for the seller to give title of the Goods as opposed to a receipt of sale.

The management of a group of people to British Law of selling titled property as Aurochs, restricts our children from ever meeting Uncle Tom. There was just too much oral discussion and not enough research on the artifacts belonging to the war office. They were written off and they became, like my paintings, a hidden trust for future generation of family members to dwell on. The truth of a building code to protect these ownerships and to not cover the towers of aerial ATCs was a loophole that the designers of the 9/11 attacks knew as hijackers to a financial account. They took their opportunity from the intelligence of the American people themselves and for me the long journey from where I began to where I am now shows the artifact and the ghost are one in the same.

The days are cooler here. Sometimes I would carry the artifacts into the field, invested in the knowledge that this is what makes me unique, unlike the forces which brought us together as school children. Hearing the classroom again in those field trips and reliving the taunting of the boy in front of her desk, she could say that she was personally stronger by using both sets of language skills. In comparison to the old neighborhood in Quebec, children there were taught to throw stones. The difference in being collectively more educated made the treaty between the two cultures a peaceful jest of fun so that neither party would be left resorting to physical violence.

The province had betrayed her though. There were old abandoned buildings where she remembered how dark it was inside. Their facades were what drew her into the heart of the designs. They were interesting and attractive at the same time. They were a reliable source of our place in history but like a broken puzzle. Today, in the newness of our working environments, I could see what made them leave seem very Rastafarian. It was a journey that gave her the sensation of vertigo for the very first time.

I kept at the public occupation concerning the psychometrics of this administration of landscape in Canada along with the childhood memories of gothic anthems to measure against her precious amulet of the soldier Raphael in her company. It is now 2008. The year of construction was 1988. From both sides of the border security, she walked the straight and narrow lineage into heaven remembering her regimental number as important. It gave her access to naming rights, thereby making the seller accountable to the goods being offered. I watched again as she furled herself upward to touch the very tip of the spire. Then the work began.

She kept her UN badge for that philosophy of encouragement in her history of firsts. Carry the burden to trust not like the banner of challenge. Just carry it for the management of our people and the price they have already paid. In this domain, there can be no attrition.

Do not accuse an innocent person. The poles of generations of social assessments were an obligation to the truth of ownership of her employment. Ensure that she is safely delivered through the Arabic signage. The treaty must include this, "Do not destroy the marriage for biblical jurisprudence. Instead, become the white rose of the letters in the angry vengeance of verging foes."

Everyone here has their matriculation. In complete opposition, there is the polygamist father. They have initiated complete political chaos in our Canadian ensign. Their nemeses are the formal adoptions of the liberal agenda for transporting men into war. When this occurs, remember that the real law forbids you to take somebody else's life as your own.

The collision repair of her accident took three days before the Markham office Mafia agent gave the name in print for the write-off and the link to title skipping. In the end Dominique, the ombudsman was unavailable for closure as he was away on holiday and there was nobody available to take the call of distress for her vehicle.

This is the investigation into why Flanders Place has two postal codes. In contrast Bishop Road has none with the Brock Boulevard and Brock Crescent as federal reserves to the paralegal office. My vote says that I doubt Point Frederick Drive very much will have reason to doubt me when I say there are two First, Fourth and Fifth Avenues here to address willful blindness. That is why there is so much controversy about the sex curriculum in our school systems. It appears the tax account can be tampered with by accessing our utilities of pensionable names in the municipality that dictates our acceptance of the LGBT community.

Two locations now to serve you the documents of entrapment. The head office systematically sheltering its publications of sexual contradiction and a sprinkler system to write off the feminine hygiene products on the shelves of employers first. When I vote I understood that it was not for social services. I thought I was voting for the leadership without dictatorial control over my children to decide which markets of employment were a choice for their stable income as opposed to police entrapments of the maternal copyright privilege of driving her children to an institution of higher education.

The laws of copyright are not attached to export or import services. They are a fact of existence. To incriminate that which is good for the economy of growth by Constables of the Municipality of the intents of the Father to a catholic base of taxation means that you are setting the taxpayer up for the debate on original sin. So, I would imagine that if Athena and Minerva were faulted as a system of respect to a cultural identity, then the soldier is a good proof for the land and the ownership of those lands.

The element of vengeance to endangerment with the seat of an aircraft to those of a motor vehicle is the truth to a construction model. Political consequence was the Parliament to ensure fearless knowledge. We were supposed to envision a better future for our children than those which caused the destruction of Troy. If making the best goods on old debt means making dirty bombs, then I see the person of incriminates the female soldier in a religious creation of false documents is a fraud and should be removed from their jurisdiction immediately since they are so busy stabilizing the tax rate for their buddies in the penal codes that the birth rights become just a fete champetre.

There is no mechanical labor for births. In a world of engineering processes, I can see there not being a wanted investment into the naming rights of mothers to their children. Where there is no C in Arabic, Hebrew, Greek or Russian languages, the C is a sign all Canadians need to be protecting in this world of technological hackers. I used it to remind the public of the fact that we belong in a beautiful world even though the obeli is a sign of the brother's keeper. It should be made a gift of leadership to those of us who are grateful to our country and its parental inspirations of lineages to the Folly Lake of satellites exposing the rose as it builds on the royalty of these writings which are a base to a different type of study to the land. It is my opportunity as a taxpayer and owner of an ensign that is small under the protection of the great.

There is no way I can rid the world of every dervish business activity. Nor can I personally expect the world to be rid of all evil and poverty. The privilege afforded to me in the clear conscience of the Forgiven Soldier is a morning side of the greatest free will gesture of all, the letter C.

It is the chapter in a book. It is a metric measurement for commerce. It is the colour of nothingness if it is not endless darkness. It is the coin in establishing the money account and the consent to the Captain of the Guard. It is the cord of the natural falling off to the word Abscission to a seraph of light embedded in a bevel of crystal that is captured from the corner of our eyes. We are still resolute among the questions that remain in all that we have studied, and we are not exchangeable to the folly of normal prudence to criminal behaviors to risk the lives of our children for the future wellbeing of our country.

CHAPTER THIRTEEN

SEQUENCE OF NUMBERS

In an idyllic sense of writing, there will be sea lavender to support our cosmos. Land, sea and air are reflected images that stand for our government to have a navy, army and air force with its own set of social rules and an equal opportunity to participation in those careers should not be made absolute by the garnishment of wages in a dower of inappropriate charitable organizations. In the artist's single moment of tenacious understanding, I can be the author to the memory of this epiphany of colour. In the essence of contract law, it is not just the expression of etymological discovery outside the catholic empire of burdensome crosses, it is the definition of a land that is unusable made usable in the shape of wood, stone, and elements of metals. Even the plush floating of our icebergs are reminders of the sizes of freestanding megaliths that are as spectacular as the mammals which occupy that same sense of home to our survival.

My house and its ghost have been found. It is a system of logistics and a balance to the development of the command for navigation and safety. Transcendental mobility is the guarantee against a neurosis of expressions from the orator of published letters. In this inheritance, St. Matthias was chosen by lot after the Ascension to take the place of Judah. As reasoned with the Mayoral candidate, this would be an important undertaking for the Ahmadinejad since oil paintings are specialty goods. The galleries are managed by the commissioned artists. There is no threat to all things being true of the final presentation. We understand the security without repression or guilt. In the contractual definition, the quality made the supply work.

In this area of Canadian history, Stacey was the first appointed Canadian Army historian who had books published by both the King's Printers and the Queen's Printers in Ottawa. Stanley became chairman to the history department of Royal Military College which supported the integration of Canadian provinces equally. The name Barker is the piece of fabric embarking on the RCAF with Ministerial approval. If in the case that there are no ownerships to anonymous resources, then the numerator becomes the yea and the denominator becomes the nay. For example if the ratio of yeas to nays were 3/2 to the eighth degree or 26 times two, then the ratio is 52 percent for the management to base their analytics on the success rate for the shift in resources of a company to realize the economic benefits of useful resources. It was also shown that with the shifts in materials only, that there were only ten combinations giving the human choice over that of the computer. These numbers were found to be 4/3 or 20 percent, 5/4 or 12 percent, 6/5 or 8.5 percent, 7/5 or 30 percent, 7/6 or 7 percent, 8/5 or 86 percent, 7/8 or 6 percent, 9/7 or 15 percent, and 9/8 or 5 percent to the approval of shifting in relationship to the success of a company for the long term of market place activity.

Since art plays a vice-gerent member in good standing, the ethics of intention verses the ethics of responsibility underlies the assets in such a manner as to apply the factory patents to its financial terms. In human resources, the creative virtuoso rule of thumb rates the equality of employment minus the equality of results as a number greater than zero. Decidedly cooperative, if it had not been for her to simultaneously equate the ethics of intention to the ethics of responsibility as zero in number, their loans would have been recalled. As the consequence to the accounting system, which divorces everything mathematically, since nobody could be just one number, the hidden gate to an eternity was found to be a changing force.

Beware of the multiplier effect. The signing authority changed with the command every other year. So, if you do not heed her carefully placed penny weights next to the 24 June, you will succeed in doing nothing more than to exalt a spoiled child to cry wolf all day long for the legal team. To prevent this, we have fixed short-run distances contingent for the penny royal.

I don't believe in ghosts. However, when the burden of the published penology goes so far as to make self-incrimination a peoplehood, then the elections of licensed drivers from outside the Mayoral district of councilors might as well be prepared as an underground economy with the pentacle their magic absit omen. If for real, we have the group of nations working inside its perimeter. Just like the dilemma of who is the first born of biblical intervention is the names Angela and Ashley for the beginning and the end.

Justin is another example of a name that means a peoplehood for the 24 June. The contribution is for the priests of electronic transfers of money. Shredding the Alleen logo was going to be difficult since the brotherhood is not really a brother. I didn't have to be protecting everybody's interest, just those who were a reasonable respect to be my home address. As military people movers, despite the bickering in Parliament, the term partisan is derived from those election promises as though they are a fictional new release.

The proletariat is depending on the capital for selling his labor. If they are attached to the tax base, they will work the pennant flag in commission. That is the reason for the change in command. Yet if you are stuck in the middle, you had better devise an exit strategy. The snowflake was clearly the Ascent from the Coup d'état. This is what made the artist different than the retirees. If you have Athena, they can't claim you for Minerva. When the accident occurred, the Teresa would have been that calling for the bid of fields of excellence. The artist was anything but the Minerva and there again we have protected our flag with the contribution to property and a management of certificates to our careers.

I understand only too well the paradox of the letter character service to the Ms., Mrs. and MR Holland. It is nothing more than Psy ops. SI units are used in the jargon of engineers, not electronic communications which entrap the victim of a crime to the tax rate of criminal minds to the expert occupations of military service administrations to their academic protections against the Phoenix of parental dragons.

The purple is real. This is not a statement created by me. L.M.M is the first to have penned that phrase. However, I use it to construct a motivation for the subject of an oil painting which saw the "Silver Thaw" to the depths of depression by the death of my own mother by the QEII Health Sciences Ctr. As the master of the work to her known music of eighteen signatures for each bar and six lengths of notes to sign in any of the four clefs, it was for sure a sign of something great. I don't think there was enough evidence for the actuary to quibble about the incorrect spelling of just one word to condemn her soul to an eternity of servitude. It is not the hardware that rests with the end user. It is in proving that the invisible could be made visible. So now I have the pleasure of informing anyone who reads even just a small portion of these dots on a page, that the invisible is real. The ghost is the seal which was placed on our accreditations. We have paid the most and we have received the least amount of gratitude in the end for our maple leaves of our uniform and oaths.

The kings walk here before our children and the litigious of the fallen are lead free in a beautiful clear silver thaw morning in the province of the Appalachian Mountains. As a Canadian artist, every one of the names transformed are based as a crossing of the Abegweit authentication to her vigil. Her light was found along the Journal Pioneer stories of the accident which claimed her daughter to the world of the ephemeral that hang in her atelier of hours spent while in attendance to the Praseodymium people casting lots to exchange their sisters years of birth from 56 and 58 for a 59 percent vote ruling of the capacity to hire him.

The soffits are not the sophists of every ability of man to perform on the public stage. The residence of hindsight is the same residence of foresight for what we requested and requisitioned. The supply has safely arrived. In curvilinear theory, the classical model is not an arrow to outrun the target practice of the RCMP patrol. Similarly, the Despatch is not a regimental support of the Royal 22nd based in QC Citadel history. We are the copyright to a newspaper whereby the signature is a choice to a military placement at the end of the line of Honourable Speakers.

We have created opportunities in a country where Antigonish is both the country riding and the Town's proper name in the study of Atlantic geology or AG not Ag. Milton is next to Shelburne in that same province where we studied the tides of old sailors who've rested here for a short time like the Manes of old women. We've been to Bell and back again for the last four decades. The rest is not for me to forgive in the pastoral mind of the A5 survey to the name of Dr. Richardson.

Janus masters the last. She too was asked to leave for her conceit of the Eastern Passage home to my children's safety. The axis of the Monk to the Viscount obelus is not the Ob of the Russian river. Oblong is geometrically described as deviating from a square to a rectangle with adjacent sides unequal. The Ob river is still a very long framework for society as is the St. Lawrence to the Monk of our Canadian constitution. A violation to Section 91 and 92 has occurred on the 24 day of December 2018. The Minister who understands that praxeological knowledge of driving is an occupational code to her Department of Federal military artists to ward off fiscal restraints. The band she purchased was the definition of colours in a semicircular form like a mobius strip of cyan representations with shades of the blue-green spectrum of light transcending physical possession.

An history of the application of the hard sciences treats knowledge as a predictable function of human interaction.

This does not apply to military knowledge of the use of capital equipment and the real estate of our Parliament. We cannot predict the future. Yet where there is cooperation into the 5G network of commerce, we will see the bank notes signed in very different ways. I have the bank note signed by Governor Rosminsky as it was the first dollar earned by me when I was fourteen years old and I was very proud of the fact that I had earned this title of employment potential. Today however, we are continually being summoned by the Courts to entrap either our parents or our children by the now LGBT-Q. It is not a community anymore so much as it is a political persuasion against the ownership of property and the rights of individual personal taxation in Canada. To litigate the owners of their personal property is communism. The EU players of the integration of these Dykstras to the dictionaries of our educated classes means that we are compelled to understand the criminality of minds as a wager for addictions which complicate the character references of our wage earning mobilities. When the postings are including the furniture and effects of employees, this means that the profile of the expectations of the ownership, not those of isolated hunters would reveal the reclaiming of their property from their employers of both genders in our Canadian Armed Forces personnel as opposed to those of import customs services to asylum seeking immigration officials in Ottawa's cache of good will organizations. There was no Captain when I arrived in Ontario and without the noble office of the ensign, I would not allow my children to be confined to a gulag for the convicted strength of the bullet proof vest holders of our profiles. Canada supports the

Star of Courage and that is exactly what I needed to prevent this from happening.

For both students and instructors, the claim is to reference the difference between a teacher in the primary and secondary school system over the menorah of the stand that two persons are required, by law, for every vehicle in operation. While only one driver, once licensed, can operate the equipment at a time, the reality of one person being an employee and the other being a family member shows how categorically the ECCs and CFRs are important to the CD recipient.

Since I did make the trip there and back from the fabled Seaking helicopter crash in Norfolk, VA and in time to be on parade, the local police had no right to use undue pressure of their male bondage handcuffs to contribute to an infraction of our Canadian Constitution and to further add the insult of writing that personal slander of the person herself, to her ownership of property is a violation of the City to the safety and security of every person, whether employed by the City or not. The international driver's license and the CAA insurance were declined as Claire did not have any such provision when she died on the Autobahn. We still don't know if she came back to Canada at all physically from Germany. In the social agenda of persons born, Shinea with the obelisk, had no basis for constitution. She was under two years of age and not old enough to conclude her sister's bias to being Canadian or not.

The sculpture of my included ensign is for the number 0 for the year of conception. In that sequence, I still would have been twenty and not twenty-one when arriving for military training where my sister could never have accomplished what I had for the protection as mother to my children.

He, the father of all unwed fathers, was of the occult and knew the sequence of men over the service of women to draw on our CRA accounts of residential postal codes. Everything we purchase commercially is a trademark, except for the stone in the form of a spadix. English terminology of the Latin species for lands might appear differently for the certification of University, College or Secondary School Graduates for the written speech as opposed to the oral agreement to attend a wedding ceremony of the family lineage with an ownership to the Isle of Ireland. The basis of my painting to show possession to Canadian art was the letter X which forms the artifact of the intended use of the focal point to the viewer. The subject's landscape proves the daughter as a graduate to a University degree with no attachment to the weighted Brian and his claim to his only granddaughter. Stated again is the fact that an IUD is very different from the IED and the DNA associated with the Monarchy of Ghosts in the house is a willful intent to defrock this artist of their rightful ownership of their lands here in Canada. The Warford of the Newfoundland regiment would have helped cause the Wedge between mother and daughter for the Armida canopy of security

depicted in the character "Cidillia."

I named the character to dismiss the Opus Dei to the single letter currency posted at the sentry to the folly of getting away from her father's curse. The declaration of independence was made in 2011 and not in 1979. It was without interring generational conflict such as the Army General to his President that assumes control over the conflict of the Middle East. The E of the mail system was carefully monitored so the compliments had to be served to the logistics officers and not the communication's officers.

Never leave your buddy in the hands of the enemy.

She received the silver butter knife with the number 18 to the southwestern storm that struck the history of Clinton, AB. In the Victorian sense of this being a staple good from the rations provided her grandmother during the war years when her husband was away and her daughters were at the sensitive age of being teenagers, I was very honoured to have this to add to the collection of growing artifacts to the history of our country. In comparison to the Dr. Ansul of the medical team in the distribution of military ambulances, the designation of a 24/7 system was very much showing the crow's nest of ownership to one's copyright.

A countermand force is required against the act of war. The threat was exactly a Rockwood to the emblem of Newfoundland made into an England tourism gift brought back by her boss from the 1 Field Ambulance of Calgary for looking after their house's contents while they enjoyed a family vacation. From the list of events in Confederation and the deployment of military postings, was a trust to allow everyone to be afforded a vacation after working all year long to secure our nutrition and our sovereign. Although it did nothing to protect the public's knowledge of death and taxation by legal legislators for promoting the 303 Street addresses for the School of Business. The third leg of our equation to the table of building codes used to barter our vacations was the capacity to hire beyond the age of forty-four. This was to reference the 6 June as opposed to the license number AKYK 477 and AD405. That campaign was an illegal write off for the political scalper.

He tried to write off his spouse with the truck number. Then he tried to divorce the situation of CPP to be signed over to him every month so that she had nothing to live off in the economic relationship of an home address to the gravestone purchased for his grave. The next target was Blaize, despite her absolute obedience to the law. Diane was the accounting mistress to the autobiographical sketch. She is a transfer to the Royal Bank. While although the BNA is no longer the same document in existence, the fact that the interpretation of every province as to the ownership of lands in economic crisis was not supposed to be a summons for the Hollywood sales of vacations into the American monetary system.

The monetary system of Cardinal watches has always been a plus or minus along the quadratic intersections of vehicular accidents. Here land selling for only the policy suggests that she was the preference to take advantage of for the dowry so that he could later curse the ground you walked on. Is this land sealing the second generation to the obligation of oblates?

I am the artist with a studio in direct conflict with the returning officers of military campaigns whose siblings do not have the same districts of ownership that we do for showing the atheist of victims of increased alterations to their uniforms of retirements. The investment in the compatible interests proves that the substitute mother, nanny, was an overrated position for the mainstream economics of our biological ownership to the first name with the CD order of merit. From this understanding, I cannot realize the hostilities involved in the psychological path of the Electra and Oedipus combat situation with the names Esau and Jacob.

It took me two days to put together this show for the wanted display of the public show to my art. It was supposed to be a support for the consensus of a copy of Feynman's Rainbow available without a library attendant. It is not the same thing as tabling a license number BAMT 949 for the Whig story.

The classification of the unwed mothers is or can be religiously extremist for the case in point for the unemployed, orphaned and the widowed. Here in my case of history to the province of my joining confederation is a Barker, VC who will never be a Bishop. The T could not be bought for the price of a G. That is a year of rights in context with the contents of this manuscript which could not be made responsible for the signatures of the Mormon administration and like the point made here could not be integrated with the Monajemi of the Moslem faith. My crown is acknowledging the Soldier ON: Quiznos or Couseneau sound very much alike which is the problem with language taken in the oral tradition. The listener may hear something different in the accent or inflection of the words being delivered. Could the bombing of Hiroshima or Nagasaki be prevented?

In the discrimination of AI to the licensing of women in the Canadian environment to the military occupational codes be any different than the oral tradition of our elders as allies? Valentine's Day is no different from UN Day except one is in the calendar month of February and the other is in October. A religious iconography is no different from the abstract of the political sabbaticals to constitute the number of students to candidate the PHD using the disrespect for our military services collectively to their ownerships. The cost of a police station is around the 60 million mark with the Federal departments of land surveys as part of the purchase agreement.

Cataraqui means rock rising out of the water. Here spouses cannot testify against each other in the court system which is why the constables would use family law to divorce an economic condition on any common law partner within the organization of police reports and the interpretation of what constitutes the official capacity of legal security agent when they are using numbers which are corrupting the real values of a security threat.

Women should be protected against police slander and willful threats to their ownership of land. A church's hierarchy and a synagogue are both liberal men.

I say this because my father made a long-distance call here to my place of employment to say that his only son had done his thing meaning that he was going to be a father now too. In the Holy Ireland of our family bible, there is an interest in this knowledge from the construction platform of the land. His wife, not an absolute personification to the name Mary, also shows how my brother is not the personification of Jesus. The absolute personification of the man though was the financier of the building to which his son and wife would be living. For the Tulchinsky of the year 1949 to the Newfoundland of joined confederation, I could hear the statement of hatred as clear as if it were a real statement out of the father of his father before him. "I will put enmity between my seed and thine."

Ownership is an interest in the antiquity of a community. In the English Scotia Minor of my texts, Yeats with the obelisk was the first Senator to be awarded the Nobel Prize and I wondered what year his daughter would graduate in order to be a peoplehood to the Breadlebane number 18 of residential details to the Meacham atlas.

My uniform is a guarded mainstay for the independent spirit that disciplines the Gardner. I have no Sisters Uterine or German Whites. The infinitive is non conceptual. He knows his commerce very well and thus he knows the psychology of these writings in manuscript form where Cardinal is a red of war. Elanoides Fortifications is an aerial bird of prey in northern climates. It is an index card for the series of arrangements to the logical requests in a static environment called a school of instruction. The people are inclusive of the money supply in banking, not the Communications and Electronics Museum exclusively to the mecca of Military ordinances. Bryce York knew what we both saw from our sources of tax implications and the measurement of time. The difference between his inflated ego and my hat badge was that I still honour my name and my uniform. It can never be made self incriminating. The badge is carried with me in a show of peace in the intergovernmental organization called Confederation.

The A5 entries into the artist's collection have no expiry dates. As an artist, I believe we have environmental changes to deal with as well even if our governments work slower than we do. I am convinced that doing business with the masculinity of all people would be like doing business with a series of totalitarian poverty driven user manuals. My William is the proof of the standard celebration to our achievements in life where the Major Blais with an obelisk died at the youthful age of thirty-one.

CHAPTER FOURTEEN

CERTIFICATES MERITS PAY

Apolune is the development of the old clock. Rose fish is the red fish species found in the North Atlantic waters. Roshi is the spiritual leader of a community of Zen monks in the Japanese culture. Nire means near. The padlock law contained the contemporary landscape in Quebec. It took the Kabinett to a different level of occupancy and it required a new form of residency. The politics of the cedar knows no boundaries here. The tree has already been felled.

So, what can be finer than cheating on the alewives in living standards or even out of their inheritance as the economic crisis blames the world for not turning fast enough. Fire regulations were not meant to develop a basis for communal living. The capital budgets set every year with the command of the DA holders meant that women were written into the Liberal agenda as though they had a religious dowry identification to dower a monarchy of the Holland fatherland of public account.

In remembrance to the accident of my calling card was that there were no pedestrian crosswalks on Granville Street. As far as I know there still are no crosswalks. The facts to the investigation from the eyewitness should show that the vehicle moved across both lanes of traffic before returning to the heading of south bound and in a field approximately 2 meters from the edge of the road. The decision to determine the safety of ourselves should not have been turned into a game of thrones by the lawyers at the time of setting a trial date. That vehicle in any category of vehicles was an historic marker for the Ministry of Transport as a people mover. The legal team went on a power trip within the decision for the destruction of the credibility to the facts. It was systematic administrative discharge in an area of institutional religious hierarchy for at least one of the pedestrians.

The secret log of replacements later on for her own family could never physically happen so only a financially induced psychology to protecting the procreation of men up until their children reached the age of sixteen, the age of voting rights, and to then destroy the family unit by bastardizing their children with the social insurance number system.

This story had to be big enough to allow the chaos of being taken out of the secondary markets for the military ensign with its mobility of people to show that the investment in her education was a better retreat than the feudal system. If government wanted to make shifts in their resources to meet an ever-changing demographic of world leaders, then it was just as important to protect the military from their public service employee attempts at excommunication of their wages when being transferred between military bases. Logistics requires knowing whom your business is involved with since logisticians do not act based on faith alone.

The Newfoundland Tobin knew what she was doing getting involved with a married man. The result of a bastard child to be broken between the shared interests of neither the notion of a mother or father shows the child as a ward of the courts. This could not happen to the William of our VC awards to the history of naming rights.

Working as an aftermath to those who have been tried by the legal status of both victim and challenger to the aviation industry, the two men who received vasectomies from the military lineages of last names did so for accepting the catholic practice. I could only reason this with the fact that if mammals and fish can share the same ocean without the destruction of the balance in nature, then why is it that we cannot be more accommodating to the protocol of homeownership without destroying the universe? The women and men who testify against the witness were also testifying against the God of Israel.

For all that which was done and cannot be undone, I will not deny the existence of God or the right of leadership among those who follow this path. The only condition I wanted to see changed in the constitution of my own mother's life, was to make sure that leadership was an opportunity for both genders and not just the authority of the Pope. It took the remembrance of that additional factor of investigation into my own career and husband to see that the roads Granville Street and Pope Road were not always a part of the survey plans to Prince Edward Island.

The report against the telecommunications services to boast that the accident was her fault, linked the ISO with her CPP and the OPP of negative GMTs. Thus, it was shown how she accomplished the showcase of the name Brian to the Holy Ireland of cremation services. His only daughter as the attachment to a ministry of vital statistics is a fraud in the form of a Grant to the brotherhood of electrical workers. The IBM Crastina of threats here to the name of Roy is still a begrudging assurance of gentile penitentiary inmates to the most unclean interpretation of revenue minister garnishments.

Looking at the reality of threats to the homeownership of these institutional protections was not a threat from the past but more the reality of being prepared for slaughter along with the cows from the same institution. That is why she questioned the deliberate exchange of industry codes from within the revenue commission to account for the payroll of nanny services to the title of the artist. On behalf of the City of Realtors of closure to the sales, what was really at stake with the intimidation of licentious pagan leaders with the ownership of land for a Captain title was instead a titled Chief of Police to verify all Ford vehicle activity while investigating the ownership and accountability to categories of vehicles using municipal parking lots.

The old man indeed did use her broken ankle to allow a mafia style association to the freelancing of its henchmen when it came to the international corporate structure of airport airbuses. The name Norman Rogers to the codes of air travel destinations proves that retirement sex is accounted for within the clinical research study at Queen's University of Goodes classification of Escheat possibilities. The LGBT-Q political rally is an example of how the Mayor of any City proper is out of control with their leadership of its taxation and ownership principle. The result is expropriation of land to use the telecommunications industry of reality TV to convict innocent people without a fair examination of the facts. It is corrupt and abusive by all men in society. Yet, when it comes to saving lives as a repayment to the kindness of others have shown to you when you were felled from an accident, then there should have been no person alive today who should be allowed to raise their hand against the author of this manuscript as a Judah of chauvinism would be for the cross of the assembled.

The maple leaf of her Canadian CD medal is not the red cross of St. George. That philosophy is the logarithmic neurosis of the Navy Chaplains to the confinements of the general tax bracket and the debt of the government to pay for its legislature. If the artist is being tested on the land we use to display our colours, then I personally would have to reject the occasion of contractors to Moncton the introduction of Hellenism to the minds of children. Wiesel knew very well the Mohamed destruction of women. So, this Abegweit story will be a link to the history of Canada instead of being the hypocrite involved with the Augustinian Monks. To all things known, there can be a new beginning and to create from those beginnings is to delve into the very pores of existence.

Belligerence is premeditated. It is used by people who abuse their authority as a status symbol of blood relations. Ruth was the wife of a Lasure circumstance of reports to details of military DA holdings to vehicle activity both on airfields and in a theatre of war. Their assets, that were once a debt, were rebranded to be profitable for the public view to the history of our Western Abenaki. This was a comfort to the cancer that is like losing every girlfriend you ever had.

I could never be that much of a hackle to the uniform of my colleagues and I could never be that forbidden as to be a Jane Doe in the jargon of the Bindi forecast. Make sure your wife does not get criminalized for obstructions on the roads. The jones is the fixation for the Liberal agenda and on Federal property it is a risk far too great for the protection of our children. Hegel warned of this form of political liability when it came to the enforcement of minority governments as though they were in joint custody after a divorce.

My scars were real. Theirs were the results of a self-imposed Mercer in commonwealth seniority. Confederation has returned a social justice alert in the avatar of vehicle destructions. Commander Chanter has not seen the Matiasso of the TM visible in the diction of arranged marriages when the children are born out of a wedded involuntary circumstance only to have a second chance at the birthing experience. A copy of her existence still exists in my discomfort of past experiences with the seal of a letter from NATO – not NAFTA signatories of world religions.

I have never asked anyone to do something that I could not do myself with the condition of the crown on my shoulders. From that framework, there will be no cannibalizing of vehicles for our driving records. The social contract for the TM was broken before we arrived at the terminal. Do not trust the Shakespeare Irving who was born John Henry Brodribb. It was only a matter of time before they would start to claim their own organs as a list price for carrying charges. The Gabriola package of the end of the month of December was the anniversary to claim and not their birthrights.

My sister, as an emplacement against the artist with her use of illegal drugs, could not use the manpower of emerging technologies to write her out of the book of life. Likewise, the illiterate link to the Mormon emigration was not going to erase the qualities of certification to the CD and the

ABD. That is why I took the heavy equipment training to the table of debate. I also saw the Armida as the antithesis to Kali. This division was the difference between gerontology and gynecology in the development of individual choices to their spouses without the early childhood education of Catholic School Boards to compromise the security of their single dwelling home. To sum up the danger involved in the fathers of confederation, do not use my father's name as your own for the classification of commerce and its profits.

The contract was out of our hands now that the commissions are not unionized medical facilities. In a consort with the facts now, the club had its own constitution and the representation has an elected delegation to the tax collector for a fee which pits the courts against the free will to be able to walk across the street without being solicited by the local police for the maintenance of its parks, statues, bridges and traffic symbols. The matter of the use of money for infrastructure that has no collective ownership for the insurance of policy owners is a use of numbers that should not be abused for the purposes of entrapments by the secretary to the Mayor stating that the Old Bill is too big for her to pay.

Building code occupancies are required to be updated and the brokers knew who and when to trade their clients. The replacement policy means to stay away from Ambulance Services. They are like borrowing books from the library: it doesn't cost money at the time of borrowing; it costs when the item is returned late or not since it costs for the digression of assurances to the truth. Without the facts relevant to a person, books probably will sit on a shelf with no one to read them anyway until the next teacher assigns a topic of research to their innocently recruited law students.

The cost of borrowing money on debt was their biggest problem associated with the Ravenview plant. Where trains are a strategic resource, the request for an ambulance would have to be declined. The cherub of her child's autonomy is not acting in defense when she is struck by a vehicle, she is trying to piece herself back together with the number 18 for the Defence of our medals of honour to the public purse. I am sure the last thing she wants it to hear is the equality with which all men are born.

Publishers can be Administrations for the Canadian trophy case. Also, by knowing which way the river is flowing is a vital component in the security of the command of navigation and safety for the fur trading ancestors of glacier deterioration. British car manufacturers are the same as aircraft manufacturers of engines. The responsibility of their OEMs is not in the end use so that the UN contracts that are worth one billion at budget, may be worth two billion to the end users of its capital. This is how we have created a rift in the economy of Crown commissions and the financial markets to a fair priority to the election process of government medical conditions.

So how can we beat the MPs of recession? The Prairie needs federalism in its structure in order to maintain our sources of primary markets. The government required capital to maintain our security and the threat of our safety as individuals to a communities' profitability. Having continuous discord with the value of wages for her delivery of fuels to foreign aircraft by the value of the American flag to the superior dollar conversion ended in the discrimination of her air force blues with the attrition of the Land Central Forces Majors on our Parliament Hill offices. In the absence of a Captain, I had to hire myself to get rid of the political rivalry staged between the military ensign and the public service administrations to a Presidential candidate of Empire Life reinventions of the wheel. Certainly, the license plates were different when the vehicles purchased changed their category of ECCs. I chose colour over luster.

Niggle means to irritate and I can quote the subject matter on the mud flaps of the kilometers traveled to determine my lineage with my children. When it occurs without the third person, keep an inventory for the financial biology that is both urban and rural. This way you cannot be eliminated by the telephone directory services. If no harm was noted, no forgiveness is required. I was the first of the siblings in the A5 framework. It doesn't matter how much cloud space is used for the proposal of a bunker, the trailer, as storage, would replace the harvest month of Sukkot commemorating the wilderness. In recognition of significant events in the solar panel design to produce electrical power on remote grid requirements, the land is already a fair wage for labor.

The condominium may never be paid off even though the business supports the staged commerce of either A or B. The meeting format is Part, Section, Subsection, Article, Sentence, Clause and Subclause. It is always this way for any directive of vocational building training. Sentence 1 of Article 1 of subsection 2 of section 2 lists the description of an event of risk or injury to the resistance to unwanted entry caused by intruders forcing their way through locked doors or windows whereby the occupants are unable to identify the potential intruders as such.

This was the situation this family was confronted with by the City of Kingston from a whole host of political evangelicals. My daughter was made to deal with the probability that the building will be exposed to unacceptable risks of damage via threats to fire safety systems failing to function as the expected age of majority approached. The functional statement as the "Afterword" to the subdivision approving by-law office might have been a casement of shells used by either the rifle range or the skeet shooting locations to her parent's military knowledge or GSK. It was lucky enough for me to be the owner with enough ability to notify persons of the need to act in an emergency. The cost to rectify the problem of fire safety regulations was eight thousand CDN dollars.

The biggest mistake the Attorney General's Office made for the province of Ontario was not realizing the capacity to a logistics statement that I don't need to taste an oyster to know what an oyster is. The education of our children to be secure with reference to the taxations paid by the ownership should not be tested by every non profit organization to doubt my ability as a sane discussion on gender without argument through the Court's system of issuing social insurance numbers for voting migrations of our children to enlist the defacing of my military salary where I have the ability to articulate clearly the duty to limit or accommodate dimensional change. The ownership here is for every Canadian to be paid for their contribution to the disciplined study which accomplishes the ABD for their family. In that same construction of ownership to property is reaching for an endless song to supply the truth to the negative experience by the misogyny of the Arabic DC as opposed to CD.

War is a mind-altering experience which both genders of soldiers are forgiven. Police are not. I know that in today's circumstance of one over the other, one does not actually need to know how to tie their shoelaces together. We see this as a division between the illegal and legal distributions of electrical codes. If you don't know the difference between an order and a motion of privilege from the ownership of the bar service, then you don't deserve to be sitting at the same table of voters to celebrate the victory over death. On the one hand I have the Massey lecture and on the other I have the Vanier French language. Both are different requests of the Rideau Hall of Governor Generals. The Megalodon was sculpted to bring the importance of unity in dither of election results across the country called Canada. The art is what is carried to show the importance of the manager of titles over the general manager of foreman power generating stations such as the Bell logo to exchange the coach's athletic NCCP sports members with those of the professionally trained military driver's coverage of titles to conclude the stations of the cross.

Since that dispute, I have since learned that perspective as metaphor is a sign signifying a mental state in the culture of fountains. Societal simplicity is a personal constant. Where the kangaroo court is a dispute in a club, make sure there is truth in death. If there is a poem for the family of aviators, make sure it is not a Creed of antagonisms to the international boundary of GMTs like Israel or even to the philosophical question of what it takes to be given a name only to have to fight for the rights of so many other people who are using the same Bell logo against you.

It also doesn't matter whether you agree or disagree with the points made on a compass. I know what is my property and I can prove that with its copyright in the exit strategy of my life. In terms of the world capacity for genocide, the odds are the same today as they were yesterday. We are lucky to have studied law in the history of Government and to discuss openly the conditions of conflict between English contract law and French Civil law. Economics is what gave most Canadians the basis of the definition of a business. If in the case of misfortune of being dropped off in the middle of nowhere, you would be capable of starting that same action repeatedly. As the artist that fits this description, I can't be the athlete at the same time for the kappa of a system of letters. Economics is also the system designed to control excesses in resources and for the system of account to control and the means of employing these same modes of production capacities. It is a proof as to the management as a tool and not a form of entrapment to the biology in the title of a President.

Health services are inelastic. It is the "Red Card" of every economic action plan. I work for a registered industry number and in that management of those finished goods is the legal consent of selling those conditions outside of the York of Cardinals' authoritarian boundaries. The price is set according to a construction in linear dimensions where each and every production is an original work of art. It is not an engineering process of existence.

The legal office of the CD Smith to sell the long-term accommodation of the family to imperfect rental conditions in Toronto was the proof of the how perfectly healthy minded children are persuaded into the plots of political debates using the historic names on schools such a Pierre Laporte Middle School. I don't need an actuary to the ties of civilized countries to see the fault in the jurisdiction of jurisprudence to my children of aviation industry to those of the army engineers. It furthermore is not the fault of a single mother to voice the concern with the foster parent's plan of impractical retail industry. We don't all want to be involved with vacuum tubes of excited molecules. Lord Willingdon was a well learned scholar for the presentation of Parliament. If the number on a building reads correctly for the Ministry of Health and in the same building the Ministry of Attorney Generals for the constitution act of 1981, then the principle of the rule of law should actually realize the judgement against the illegality of certain substances on those premises by their employees. While it may be unheard of to suggest a gender bias, it is not invoiced or unobjectionable from the odor of the item in hand to determine the difference between a cigarette used for solicitation with that of a joint of marijuana.

The polygamist cult in our country has been reported many times. The dangerous assaults made by the fathers of this cult target the female in a sexual confrontation which is also an ISBN to the library of urban religious culture. Its competition creates a kind of neurosis for those of the community not knowing of its assault against the good people of the educated and legal business classes of any province or territory in Canada. The acts of Parliament may be amended and renumbered by proclamation by the Governor General under the Great Seal of Canada which is held in secret by the Minister. The seal bears witness to the Canadian Armed Forces persons with the Distinguished Service. It does not condition the gender from which the power is essentially driven for my Codicil as a female or male receptacle. The bill is NZ2372254 who was the trained driver for the security of Princess Margaret during her Royal Tour in the province of Alberta. As an elected community service, I have provided that same security of respect for my own children.

CHAPTER FIFTEEN

UNTIMELY REGISTRAR GENERALS OF CANADA

Postal addresses in Canada always start with a capital letter. Ottawa uses the National Defence Headquarters to conduct its business with the perks of a whole association of military employees from the MGen. George R. Pearkes Building in the National Capital Region. Every gargoyle that is found in the region is brought into the writings of our military electrical codes for the enforcement of weapons used by tactical deployments either as RCMP officers or combat soldiers. The difference is that the police units can allow their members greater systematic leniencies for their smaller units than what can be obtained by the overall resources used by the structure of personnel development for long service and good conduct by members of our Canadian Forces CD medal recipients.

There is a control of documents which allows military members to use the authority of the Queen for the National Defence Act where all legal addresses published are in Administration, Disciplinary and Financial Orders. In addition to these orders, there are Canadian

Force's Administrative Orders, Supplementary Orders, Air Command Orders, Group Orders, Base Standing Orders, Base Routine Orders, Unit Section Orders and Dress Regulations. When it comes to the investigation of an infraction of harassment and a member is requested to assist with the investigation, one must fully understand the security involved with the identification of information and our property that is essential to the welfare of its participants from being compromised by police units which are gender biased to the single geographic locations of one city their entire career.

In law, there is a condition of willful abandonment for one's children if that individual is apart from their partner for longer than a six-month time period. The reality of having that happen or not shouldn't have existed by strict adherence to the exact number on a calendar. Also, as a form of reality to subversion, espionage and sabotage of a marriage when it comes to six-month deployments is the celebration of our anniversaries. A breach of the Grand Sceau du Canada is a breach of certification for the Acts of Security to the spouse of the deployed member. When information about the death of a family member is cause for a return before the deployment is complete, the inscription of both French and English, not Latin should have given his spouse the fitness award to the CFAO 2020 of the right of a citizen in good standing with the Securities Information Act for her NCCP certification and travel authorizations based on those credits. The Smith of Army Surplus in this city region are an infringement for the investigation dealing with unauthorized use of reports and forgeries of the members whose addresses are without a Sarah or a Beaton Ave to the commerce of ownership of the Christmas dinner for the boosting of morale to be served under the best conditions possible.

While although the local police have no roundel for this event, it would have been obvious to me to sense the entrapment of the mother by the intents of the essence of the Holiday Season in a constitutional death in the ownership of land and its residents to the taxpayer roll. It was a threat that was premeditated by the City of Kingston and now every person should realize the imprisonment of a crime which was not committed or ever would have been committed as a performance to the Canadian use of the fellowship of a maple leaf being inserted into the roundel.

When the phone caller asked to do business with M. Barker, then the threat was no longer without willful intent to the integrity of the daughter. The government building with the minister responsible for the Great Seal and the issuance of Social Insurance Numbers should be made responsible for the faulting of the military ethos between husband, wife and their biological parents. The report against the owners of this forgery of justice to the original sin has been prepared by the artist. The Great Seal is kept for the livelihoods of her Canting Arm as a profession of arms for the integral part of Canadian Society and her certificate of honour from the Minister of Education from the City of Summerside. She is the futuristic allotment to the comprehension of modern mathematics where she has never been arrived at an address on Beaton Avenue.

Due to these investigations, I believe there should be a revocation of the distinguished Order of the Most Venerable Order of the Hospital of Saint John of Jerusalem from the appointment of Onley. As an artist whose children know and have played the first six bars of the Royal Anthem, I believe my maple leaf was employed correctly and that the investigations into the assault on the military CD recipient is a preventable surname between 24 Sussex Drive and 690 Promenade Sussex Drive in Ottawa's electrical codes of the QEII Health Sciences Center. There was no provision for her insurance on such things as towers or aerial surveillance systems. The only thing she had was a family bible brought over to Canada from Ireland. If legal deposit is in the form of a book, mine name would be the first in this lineage of commission for Canada. It is still an honour point for the ghost whisperer on behalf of Air Command in the month of February. The difference between the Mole of the office of Escheat is that I will only be in contempt of court for a short time while he will always be in contempt for the true results of our military heritage. The image concept is not a visible financial institution to the money account of our wedge cap and air force tartan which was approved in 1942 which began on Prince Edward Island at a Robbie Burns Night mess dinner.

We have seen, as parents to this cap, the history of Europe's dictatorships. Yet the signature of paintings can be negotiated into contracts with the Capital Region to link the money accounts. The R.E.O. solicitation of a letter of law to question the Canadian flag on the file system using the name Peter Milliken to have the Holland man solicit her specifically from the Liberal party leadership in the name of John Gerretsen to small claims was a rally that is unacceptable for the contractual and hegemonic bonds of democracy.

I brought a wealth of experience and expertise to the Ministry of Education only to be given an Elaine to the story "Death on the Ice." Education is not a social program. If you are a better person than I, then why is it that the Mercer surname has to claim their political preference in the gayness on a national CBC program where the normal person in federal military professionalism doesn't even get an opportunity to claim their own footwear? As a matter of public transport, there is no Rose in my family history that has given a Massy lecture.

The poem written "Angry Little Bird" represents a Michael recorded to the address of the now obsolete 75 Clergy Street. ON the expense of my mother's headstone and my wedge cap, please do not render capable any more solicitations to ask for more money to fund the prison farms of Kingston. We do not teach our children explicit exploitation tactics. In that vanity, I am sure the Russian army would love to have you join them in Moscow. From there the zenithal projection can rival the choices of satellites to reign in the order of tactical air groups.

It is a hateful thing to assert a population's social demographics to financially institute the entire student body of one city's graduation ceremony for the media coverage of a wedding ceremony to the son of John Gerretsen. Mormons are illegal and the corruptness of using this wedding to destroy the good name of the pilot's history of the slogan, "Through adversity to the stars," for another Hollywood bash in the drug department of universal health care is a wrong PAL for the forensic accountant always being UN retired Majors for the railway caboose. Money is non-negotiable for the words, "Thou shalt not kill." My operation of heavy equipment did not carry with it the weapons of assault, so why was I brought into the discussion of gentiles over Jews or vice-versa? Was it a trade-off between the re-enactment of the history of old Fort Henry male lineages to the Speakers of the House?

It seems that when it was stated that the first is the last has been reversed to say that the last is now the first. Good thing Charlotte is between the two men. The dichotomy of Vital Statistics, not Statistics Canada, will try to prove this statement. If in the case of the twin towers, as people, one at least would still be alive to the obligation of god. As this study proved, more than one fell. And from the study of architecture from the foundations of time, the twin office towers for Congress in Brasilia are given to the hierarchy of modern lineages. So, from the perspective of my military training, I stand against being charged or held hostage by the crowds of political marijuana supporters as guilty by association to the downtown core of merchants who participate in unwanted solicitations for the crown to entrap more women with the bar. If I didn't know the facts of life before now, I certainly have had my share of training on the illegal arrests of our taxpaying properties. ATM is not a trademark and I am no Roman citizen for the Senate President. If Victoria Barker wants to be a support for that, then she will be deprived of the Sergeant with the CD2. He also has a maple leaf of which you will never inherit as the law will not allow it to pass by his only son. I also expect Rochelle will claim the same for her dad. For certain her riding will never be a burden to any military retirees of the Rochester, NY housing authorities, especially those with a NYPD badge. Colonel Coady has given his signature presentation to enforce the plates as shifting hands. Clement had the honour of the safety of our Great Seal and the Princess of my state visit to Canada is now deceased. My cameo is Air Force and our security is more than a calendar of events to a festival here in February. If you have a Cotton tale in the form of a psychological malpractice, remember that psychology is not a professional medical science.

The forest child sees the crown to the earned operations of forward operating units, tactical aviation wings and command headquarters with detachments without Scott Industrial write-offs. As for the existence of N. Baum is the fact that at the time of arrival the issue was missing the Captain for our personal protection of salaries when many employees were civilian.

Slander was the least of the torts against my person and Peter N. Cohrs had an alibi with the Mary of the occult industry. Mr. E. A. knew that he was sending this person to entrap the building of lands over votes for the office of Mayoral candidates. You can't just send an email to someone asking for a certain amount of money without a contract in place. As for fundraisers in the populations of Military College, the fact that dirty bombs for the Brown jobs of international military engagements is not what has been written into our uniformed handbook.

My defense of the number 18 was to show that I had not received any consideration for my promise to deliver him. As the driver, with my spouse, I was messaged by the people of Canada to arrive safely. That accomplished, as the artist though, I deserve remedy for the fraudulent misrepresentations by most by-law enforcements, dime bagging a law-abiding taxpayer.

If this post was to be the test of whether I understood the material assigned to my courses of certification to the tartan of the roundel, then the artist would confirm the statutory provisions to the Abegweit figurehead of the Lieutenant-General copyright 1992. As for the name Eileen, her privileges as driver will be revoked. The same situation applies to the PAL for Sam. If in fact the architect E.A. is trying to confuse the land's ownership with the Cavanah of lawyers, then the law merchant may not be a Canadian citizen at all, let alone the publisher for Queen's Printers.

The uniform is not bought through the assignment especially if the notice was not received on legal size paper or in letter form. It should be remedied as good business practice to the individual whose rights have been infringed, to use common sense when important rights are in question. His money in the tax account, could not be associated with the lands she owned and vice-versa. As the honest broker for my children, the report to the family of Toronto Noels, of which I had no prior contractual obligation with the province of Newfoundland and Labrador, to return the tax-free accounts to my children of Nova Scotia.

In the misrepresentation of the person Kimberly, not Eileen, the legal tender was the delivery of clean dry fuel to military aircraft such as the CH 133, CH 135, CH 113, CH 124, CC 138, CC 115, CC 130, CF 116, CF 188, CC 109, CT 114, CT 113 and CP 140. I doubt very much if the President of the club would ever hold these qualifications in their tenure for the offices of Queen's University Board of Directors. As for the AKYK 477, the ministry of Motor Vehicles and Service Canada do know the difference between the driver of this Cavalier brand as opposed to the Ford brands used by local police services.

In the duty of this officer to recommend, her responsibility is powered in Canada and abroad. Thus, closure in the future for the proof of her existence is a clear-cut identity to their doctrine of touching the face of God.

The amount of damages to actualizing the accident to martyr the driver of 04-31322 by the Liberal party of Canada cannot even be imagined. For sure it will be greater than the small claim of less than five-hundred dollars in favor of the meter maids. All military vehicles have been returned safe and the people in attendance became a special endorsement to the Order of Restrictive Deposit for the manuscript and record of her ownership since she did not cause the accident to occur. To raise the question in a court of law and to prevent a larger catastrophe from the licensing bureau, she had the license plates destroyed and the license number BRL-134 were to replace them. With this act of kindness to her past performance is stating that the concepts of love are an everlasting artifact to return to those who both literally and figuratively are supporting your renovation project.

The Pope should realize that he too will die, and Princess Diana will still have control over the stadiums where I have only stood to take center stage on the ablution of the inter-generational family. Luckily the sport of hockey does involve a Captain. Here he knew that the ankle did not belong to him nor to the people of Canada but what it did for the protection of the innocent when it came to charges of misrepresentation by the Ministry of Attorney Generals was providing words of motivational truths to the preference of providing associated personnel to the fulfillment of Canada's commitment to NATO and not just a Minister of National Defense.

I have maintained a disciplined occupation. It is not a matter of occasional circumstance. It is my permanent literature to realize the office of the Prime Minister as being corrupt. Kimberly, I expect, from that point of discussion on the politics of making a country, has a canopy of uniforms for the maps of federal endorsements for the protection of our current wills. Where she does not do parades anymore, the parietal bones of children are still needing to be protected. For the ladies, did you ever calculate how many more times you would have had to flush the toilet when you were pregnant. Only a real mother would have had the courage to account, with conviction, the ownership space for entitlement against sabotage to ownership in this area of municipal account. As for the Ravenview Plant, BRL-134 represents the department of vital statistics to the command transport of navigation and safety.

N stands for navy. It is the second in command for the accomplished valedictorian where drug trafficking is now the biggest sport known off the coasts of our protected waters. The sunflower trophy presented, which I anticipate is still holding the crystal orb, can never be divorced from her people since its collective is still a work in progress for the artist. Just as the name Casselman is used for the collective bargaining of unionized employees, the name Hector is also preplanning their estates where the land ownership will shift between Mr. and Mrs. They are not a crass subjugation to those people employed in the funeral services portfolio of iconic spaces with the perfected seating arrangements for the gathering of family and friends. I am not sure that there is a demand for such tyrannical public presentations and yet it may be better than hiding them inside cells of least politically involved members to the Remembrance Day services of November 11th instead of September 11th.

The mood has shifted from angry to bitter contempt for the social gathering especially if it involves sibling rivalry. Yet if the CRCT cannot challenge the disclosure of the cremation of Sam, then it is not much wonder that she would confront the President on an annual basis. In the after world of destruction in pure exploitation, she was revealed as a Muslim. To track the Fathers of Confederation to this ideologically based religion was an internet charge to providing electric bed supplies to the new Providence Care along the St. Lawrence penthouses of condominium ownerships with the signage Homestead Holdings. It is not so amusing to realize that they would rather kill you than see justice allow you entry into the next level of an accomplished pay.

The economic condition of a male over the female signature block to depreciate the publications of these military drivers is a strategy nobody could have predicted for the future condition of peace, order and good government. Where there are no scientific formulas to exercise a formaldehyde brain, the few ratios she calculated to predict the profitability of the artist was the decision used to barter the number of people reliable to getting the job done despite the conditions of following instructions to the letter. For the artist, there is no slander, no racist remarks and the harassment in the ferial span of earned time cannot be a communications and electronics senior member. Although I cannot state for certain that the Royal Commission has not already had something to do with the manner of death in the definition of an appointed manpower to the Crown investigating a particular matter, I do know for certain the economic condition does exist in reality to the Governor of the Bank of Canada where the finance minister is a sovereign representative to a bill passed in legislature.

RCMP do not have these powers today. Thus, in order to gain control over the chaos at the municipal level of both social unions between the taxation districts of Quebec and Ontario, somebody had to assign the Colonel Stacey as a similar Laurence to take away the Tims of over confidence to the franchise industry. The battlefront awards of Major WA Bishop (VC, DSO, MC, DFC), Major R Collishaw (DSO, DSC, DFC), Major WG Barker (VC, DSO, MC), Captain AR Brown (DSC) and 2Lt AA McLeod would not have seen the insignia of other NATO countries such as Belgium, Denmark, France, Germany, Greece, Italy, Netherlands, Norway, Portugal, Turkey, United Kingdom, or the United States. The Maple Leaf shared by the artist today is not interested in shared rental spaces for the protection of her entitlement to the marriage certificate.

The ability to get things done is not an initiative of these employees. Best means to be accurate and true, but not to the letter T. In the realm of competitive species, the exploration of a military leader is a journey far more difficult than the Oedipus and Electra fictional complexes. Purely competitive markets are unstable in that the result lead to a diminishing return. Conversely, public service sectors of government owned towns, cause inelastic prices with no other option for finance except to rope the tax burden among its citizens as though we are all cattle in partnership with the owners of the Calgary Stampede. If the provincial government increases taxes, then the capital of all police units will increase with the same level of deflations for the vehicle brands used as opposed to the inflationary aspects of utilities capital for the infrastructure's nonexistent land use – the electrical codes. To this end I will not be a slave to the cable of institutional governments attached to the Administration of the Wellington Street complex. It doesn't matter how much you cry for nurses. Neither will I be forced to drown in the 5G network of data consolidation without human intervention especially when you realize that Robert is the crafted name for Bob and Harold is more dangerous next to the Tiny Mars nick name of the legendary puck in Canada.

The preachers called it a book. I called it a guide. Sometimes it is visible and sometimes it is not. I decided to share in the responsibility of employment with my spouse. I also deserve to wear those rewards of accomplishment without shame for my knowing where to find the required information so that the Command knows that a correct and ethical decision was made. In this realm, there is no access pass for the building or the parking lot to the municipal library of the Mayor who made the declaration on welcoming the LGBT – now LGBTQ community to Kingston. To the office of the coroners, to be without a father and a son is an account to be self-incriminated to original sin. In that testament of the real over the physical, the soart'n letter means to get out of the debate. Grozelle, the family name, is a one point link to a host of family names to the appearance, reliability, initiative, attitude, planning and confidence in an institution that was more than a GPS of naval traditions where Nytinchyk should have realized the misogyny of the philosophy of courage: Few men are born brave; many become so through training and force of discipline. For all names mentioned after me, I am never referenced in the AD of the Roman Empire. The reason for knowing this absolutely is the fact that the ring-necked pheasants are descended from stock brought from different parts of the old world.

In Canadian industry, GDP is the employment of skills to produce in the secondary markets of production. Action is the employment of a means to achieve those ends. Not all have to be ordered by men for men or women for women. If these actions are based on instinct, not insanity, then the courts must consider the fact that an ABD must exist in the future for our economic and physical provision. He and she are not biased forms of nationalism disposing of yet another human model or mannequin of dress in the museums of College archives. I do see how the name Archie was chosen for the Prince of Wales when we see one person's vital force to protect is just as instinctive as it is for him to take aim. If we both know that we are capable of instincts just as great if not greater than other mammals, then would you not stop to question the motives of a passerby to push another off the sidewalk? What was said afterwards was said in anger.

Nationalism taken to the intestate is not good for the economy. Nameo is a Canadian first posting of the specific terms of reference to the physical reality of the security of our country. By taking off the uniform, it does not mean that people of an extreme organization can opt to vex the skill sets of the business ownership. Once realized that the A5 model was outside the Galilean system of coordinates, the physical principle with respect to 19 different types of aircraft correspond to the ECCs and CFRs of different categories of vehicles. As the manager of these reports to a command structure would realize that she was more than just another permissibility to survey the view from a more elevated position to suggest the corruptness before we even see a single bullet set in motion. To some people this manuscript is the end of formal learning. Yet to others it is a lesson most favorable to the final divisions of angels foreseen as undetectable in a remarkable destiny to the symposium on curvilinear theory.

The management redesigned the system with the command advice, "Don't move," for the army intelligence office. EAN ducked when the angel ascended.

Ingratiate Ave Identifies

Communication is beautiful.
Women strive for its excellence.
Men persist to quell its Imaginative accuracy
And the world becomes Accountable for them.

Literature teaches one
An all-encompassing moment.
Her impulses are of
Another dimension in throng, Growing like a chain
Shaping the mind.
And lyricism allows us much to see,
Outside and inside oneself
At the same time.

To imbue, she wishes for
The same saving Grace.

Apples fall off trees naturally, don't they?

"So why is everybody sounding off about this missionary position for?"

"You've answered a question with a question."

"Well at one time it was the naming rights that caused the chaos."

"Yes, so now we are back to square one with the regimental numbering system."

"Tell me, which is more important, God or the Father?"

"I think that has more to do with the air we breathe as a race; as a total entity. The oxygen is always in the air. Like politics and philosophy. Eliminate the risk of occupation. It is as ancient as history. Yet if you constitute a vessel, everyone is accountable."

"What is that supposed to mean? What is the definition of a vessel?"

"To put something in a container is more of what I am trying to tell you about and the logistics in support or rejection of those vessels. There are boats, barns, churches, malls, pill boxes: you name it."

"So, what is that supposed to mean?"

"I mean everything is time and space and money. Whichever road you're travelling, we all fall into place around this triangle of love. If somebody doesn't like you or the country you represent, they take away your breathing space. If they like you, you'll have all the government and money than you will ever need. That is why the public likes medical doctors, it's a win, win situation. On the loose, loose side, it is no different than being in the Mafia. You are told who to be married to and who gets to do the dirty work of controlling the serving of documents through a Court system."

"Ok, so what do we stand for in this scenario as soldiers to the crown?

I joined for a career."

"Yes, and I want my country again instead of being annexed to the

Americans."

"So, what are you going to do about it?"

"Assassinate the President."

"You're joking of course?"

"You know it is a fact of life that old men go crazy trying to defend themselves. President Vladimir knows that. He also knows about power. Not the power of religion, but the power to empower an army to achieve an ultimate goal of supremacy. Afghanistan is the resulting effects of such a training exercise like Guantanamo Bay was for the Americans. The only difference was how women were disposable to his ends."

"So, you still haven't answered my question of whether you were joking. How and where are the targets in this assassination plot?"

"Attrition."

"You're going to assassinate a President with the administration of retirees? Is that it?"

"Sure. The Prevost know how to reduce the numbers in the system. For God's sake, the Germans did it in the second world war with genocide. It's been done again in Bosnia. It is a common strategy to sell your command as governor-in-chief to an alien, meaning enemy Administration. Vladimir was RTU. He didn't like it so now as Prime Minister he can continue his goals. I think we're his next target."

"My wife has a number too you know."

"What's her maiden name?"

"I don't know."

"Good answer kid."

And with that Megal left the soldier to clean his weapon. He was just a private. Too clean to know military strategy. His platoon had been there for two months now and the stress was beginning to seep into their camp. Rumors are a recruit's deadliest enemy. Commissioned or otherwise, a little straight talk from the opposite sex wasn't going to hurt since the motto is always trust nobody anyway. That is professional and wise. Besides we all know our lineage anyway so why not work together for our future. She did wonder why the private used the name Sargon. As Captain, it was her job to examine every dossier to find remorseful entrants. She picked up on the name right after the group arrived. Like her, he obviously knew why it was included as a Christian name. Motivation means potential and leadership is in desperate need for motivation as an economic reality.

She had lost her dad though, through attrition. And if she had it her way, no true Canadian battalion, male or female, would be lost that way again. She had to be careful in his domain though. Soldiers are a venerated lot. Yet she still had to be satisfied at snagging this private for the show.

The day was cool, and the walk was brisk.

Sargon, she thought. Isn't that a Lord of the Rings kind of thing she thought to herself? J.R.R. Tolkien was considered advanced reading for high school entrants. Her age she thought was beginning to show through. Kids don't read books like that anymore. She remembered though a dentist whose name was Akkad and wasn't Sargon the ruler of that ancient civilization?

He was academic enough to use this name to access this war. Although the fact that he has a wife puzzled her more than the name itself. The question was, which military was he fighting for? The Middle East might be the best safe guess. Megal learned the hard way that B was for blue. The logisticians carried that banner in high regard and Megal wondered if Sargon's wife was one of those listed as dead. It was a bit out there, yet it is a crazy world here. Her own tenure as being a wife may even have been a premonition of sorts since there is no real strong religious association attached to his family history. He joined right after high school and the army needed volunteers now more than ever. She had a clearer image of her recruit now.

The base was in full operation. Only yesterday she reported on the Mongol children of the camp. They had an initial outbreak of diarrhea. Underwear was not normally worn as part of their culture especially since girls would need to be selected for sex once, they started menstruation. This was a critical situation and she watched as the matron sister gave the child a jug of water to hold until she made it to the latrine. Some of the water spilled out but the gain of making it to the latrine was worth the spoilage of the cup of water. In the dining area, an older female sat down in one of the little chairs revealing entry into the age of puberty. It was a shocking dialogue to her as a Canadian.

She quietly left the situation to demagnetize the confrontation that her presence made on these children. Somehow, she understood in some archaic way that they were all hoping for a chance to be the apple of her eye. This is what the culture of their country was like.

She stood next to the hangar doors mulling over what her next report would look like. The air was fresh, and the day was uncertain with suspense. Then one by one they began to arrive. The airborne regiment had been called to the tasking and so she started counting as they touched the ground. Their precision at landing was nothing less than expert and their professionalism was nothing short of commanding. Since time was of no consequence to anyone already on the ground, she believed it was the task of these new marshals to reset the clock on civil life.

When operations are in full swing such as this base camp, she knew the ramble to the supply office would be the requested essential service. Since she was dressed to fit in with the local diction, the run to the stores would have to be made with no shoes. She had kept a pair of totes inside her handbag. Sometimes the soldiers called it her dime bag. Yet today it was something like a diamond for her as she dashed across the tarmac, down the road and across into the stores area. The area was once a vehicle maintenance service area and the smell of oil and iron were strong to her senses. As her eyes adjusted to the dimness, her recruit caught her attention.

"There are at least fifteen that I counted."

"Darn, I said I would have underwear for all of them."

This is what happens when the supply didn't meet the paperwork for the situation and the barter system was too far removed from actual and physical reach of the obligation to provide. She knew he would be in trouble if not successful to secure the amounts without the proper paperwork. She thought about the situation for a bit and decided that there were other areas in the depot. Her recruit started searching too and both were unsuccessful in meeting the obligation of his unit's colleagues.

She understood that this was a promise which would keep our Canadians from becoming what they were like here. It may seem like nothing to a modern economy but here it was psychological. They both knew deep down how important it was to provide the garments as he said he would have available to them "when they arrived."

In an uncommon risk of her becoming involved, she went to her locker in the next building. There was a case of towels in it that was left to her by a previous drop of supplies. She grabbed the case and rushed back to give the recruit the substitute items.

His pride was in decline for not having the correct number for all the new arrivals.

"Get over yourself for just one second and you will see a different future." Megal just needed to know more about what it was that he saw to put him up there at the front of this war.

He opened the box and hummed the hymn of Jane. It was written April 19, 1836.

He replied, "Perfect peace is more important than forgiveness."

(As a matter for the history of our country and its leadership, Ariel Sharon should have initiated a solution to rename the Gaza Strip instead of destroying the settlements that were created there (Ref: Globe and Mail article written by Marcello Di Cintio from Jerusalem on Saturday, April 8, 2006 with the advertisement for Newfoundland and Labrador on the opposite side to that printed story.)

A B B C I B D B D I C D
I speak of you a ve ry spe cial friend. In memory of Cpl. Rick Hines – Fleet Diving Unit
The Right Honourable Paul Dick
CFB Shearwater-MAG

Printed in the United States
By Bookmasters